Logical Tips
for Mastering
Microsoft Office

Quick Shortcuts, Tips,
Tricks , and Techniques to
Help You Use Microsoft Office
More Effectively

Susan C Daffron

Logical Expressions, Inc.
http://www.logicalexpressions.com

ISBN-13: 978-0-9749245-6-4

ISBN-10: 0-9749245-6-3

Library of Congress Control Number: 2007909559

Warning and disclaimer: This book is designed to provide information about using computers and Microsoft Office. Every effort has been made to make it as complete and accurate as possible, but no warranty or fitness is implied.

The information in this book is provided on an "as is" basis. Logical Expressions, Inc. and the author take no responsibility for any errors or omissions. The author and Logical Expressions, Inc. also shall have no responsibility to any person or entity with respect to loss or damages arising from information contained in this book or from any programs or documents that may accompany it.

Contents

About Using Office

I have been using computers since the early 1980s. That's enough time to have seen software evolve into wonderful – and sometimes bewildering – productivity tools. I even remember the old green (or orange) screens of text way back in the bad old days.

Like a lot of people, I started with word processors. In the world before WYSIWIG (What You See Is What You Get), word processors were so basic, you often had no idea what your document would look like until you printed it.

Even primitive word processing software was a big step forward from typewriters. But here's a dirty little secret: I entered the world of computing kicking and screaming. For months in college, I refused to go to the hideous "computer center," which was really just a room with three old, weird computers in the dank basement of the library. The only reason I learned how to use a word processor was because my roommate broke my typewriter. Deadlines loomed and so I was forced to venture forth down to the dreaded computer center.

But then in the deep, dark depths of the old library building, I discovered the joys of computing. Software made it possible to cut and paste with ease. I could type away without worrying about hitting the end of the line. I could duplicate and save as many drafts as I wanted. I could print as many originals as I needed. No more carbon paper or white out!

With these early programs, if you you were careful, and knew how and where to insert the right codes, your finished document could include such exotic embellishments as boldface, italics, and even multiple font sizes.

I also remember my delight at using the first WYSIWYG (What You See Is What You Get) word processing program on an early Macintosh. That tiny black and white screen was refreshingly clean and restful to the eyes – especially after peering for hours at eerie green letters on a black terminal. On that little Mac, I stored both my MacWrite software and my paper on one small floppy disk. I could actually see – more or less – what my finished document would look like. I could even use more than one font, in multiple sizes, on one page.

Now such formatting miracles have been around for years. Changing fonts is commonplace. We have software that lets you use hundreds of fonts, draw shapes, create multiple columns, build elaborate tables, add charts and graphs, automatically paginate, construct an index, and merge names and addresses with a form letter. Software now can automate dozens of tricky tasks with ease.

You don't have to have lived through "green screen" computing to understand good software. You probably want what all of us want: software programs that make sense, do what you want them to do, and don't drive you nuts in the process. Unfortunately, the reality is that software still isn't perfect.

Software can – and will – drive you crazy, including the most popular software of all: Microsoft Office. Since I survived the green screen days, it's a bit easier for me to cope when beset with what I call *weirdness*. These tips are designed to help you deal with the type of weirdness Microsoft Office can dish out. Because most people use Word the most, you'll find more tips on Word than any of the other Office programs. However, I have thrown in a few Excel and PowerPoint tips too.

Word Tips

Now I'll share another dirty little secret with you: I used Word Perfect long before I used Word. In fact, moving to Word was a horrible transition! Sure, I later won an award from Microsoft and wrote book chapters on Word. But that's because I spent hundreds of hours figuring out Word the hard way. I got so good at it that I started sharing my Word tips with the world. After all, you shouldn't have to share my pain!

Because I've been using Word for so many years, I understand how it "thinks." At its core, Word in the 21st century isn't much different than it was in 1992 when I first encountered it.

I hope these Word tips save you time, frustration, and annoyance. Word processing should be transparent. When you aren't spending all your time thinking about Word, you can focus on the content of your document and what you actually want to say.

Word Wizardry

People often ask me how to create various types of specialized documents in Word. The irony is that sometimes a serious shortcut is just sitting there and people don't realize it. For example, suppose you want to create a calendar in Word. You could go through and create a table by hand and painstakingly format it. Or you could just use the built-in wizard.

For example, in Word, to create a calendar choose File|New. Instead of just blasting through and clicking Blank document like you normally would, look under templates in the New

Document Task Pane. Click "On my computer" and in the Other Documents tab you should see the Calendar Wizard icon. If the icon isn't there, it means that the wizard wasn't installed when you installed Word. In that case, you need to find your Office CD and click the Add/Remove icon to add all the wizards to Word.

Assuming the Calendar icon is there and working, click to select it and then click the OK button. The wizard appears on your screen. Now click the Next button to forge ahead through the wizard. First you are asked to select a design style. Pick one and then click the Next button. Then you have to decide on a page orientation and whether you want Word to leave space for a picture. Next you choose the month and year you want displayed on the calendar.

After you've made your choices, you click the Finish button and Word generates a calendar for you. Remember that it's really just a Word table, so you can reformat it just as you would any other table. After discovering the ease of creating a calendar, you also may want to experiment with some of the other built-in wizards. They are all there just waiting for you to try out.

The Best Shortcut Formatting Keys

Most people who spend a lot of time using Word efficiently soon learn about the big three keyboard shortcuts. Ctrl+X, Ctrl+C, Ctrl+V (cut, copy and paste respectively) are the best way to save time in any Windows program. But with Word, you have a lot of other opportunities to save time doing even the most mundane document-creation tasks.

Most of us can't remember the laundry list of shortcut keys in Word (or any other program). Here's the short list of the best shortcut keys to know. If you learn only these key combinations, you're guaranteed to save time.

Ctrl+X, Ctrl+C, Ctrl+V = Cut, Copy and Paste respectively. These work in virtually every Windows program. Learn them, use them, save LOTS of time and mousing around in the Edit menu.

Ctrl+B = Apply **Bold**. Highlight text then click Ctrl+B.Voila! Insta-bold!

Ctrl+I = Apply *Italic*. Same deal: highlight, then click Ctrl+I for the italics. **Ctrl+Y** = Repeat the last action. For example, say you just added a row to a table. Click Ctrl+Y to add another one. Keep hitting Ctrl+Y to add a whole bunch more.

Ctrl+spacebar = remove all local formatting. If text looks weird, it could be because you accidentally added something. It's also good consistency. You can make sure that the only formatting you apply are the changes you've set up in your styles.

Shft+F3 = Toggles case. If you know people who type in all upper case, you have my permission to rip the Caps Lock key off their keyboard. In the meantime, use Shift+F3 to switch case from UPPER, lower, and Initial Caps.

Ctrl+Home, Ctrl+End = Move to the top and bottom of a document (not a page), respectively.

Discover the Word F8 Key

Have you ever had this experience? You need to highlight some text in Microsoft Word. So you click and drag and suddenly Word seems to lose its marbles and speed up the highlighting so much that you end up highlighting four pages of text, instead of the half page you intended.

(Been there; done that.)

However, there's an easy solution to this problem that many Word users don't know. You can use the F8 key to highlight text instead of the mouse. To highlight text, click or move the cursor so it is to the left of the first character of text you want to highlight. Now press the F8 function key at the top of the keyboard. Now you can just use your arrow keys to extend the selection.

Once you are in this "extend selection" mode, you can do some tricky things to tell Word where you want the highlighting to end. For example, if you type a character such as "s" for example, the selection automatically finds the next instance of the letter "s" and extends the highlighting to that point. Similarly, you can use Word's Search feature to find particular text. So if you know that the word "canine" is on page 2 somewhere, you can press F8 to put Word into extend selection mode, then press Ctrl+F and enter canine into the Find What box and click Find Next. The text is highlighted up to that point.

After you have the text highlighted, you remain in extend mode until you do something to the selection, such as cutting, copying, or formatting it in some way. To get out of extend selection mode, you just press the Esc key, which is normally located in the upper left-hand corner of your keyboard.

With a little practice, you'll find the F8 key can save you a lot of time. It's great when you need some extra control either for selecting really small or really large amounts of text in a document. So go forth and highlight!

Timesaving Keyboard Navigation Tips

Have you ever wished you could select a tabbed column of numbers or a vertical chunk of text in Word? Maybe you thought you had to select each item separately because you couldn't highlight just one column without highighting other areas. What a pain!

Guess what? You can select text vertically in Word! Just click at the beginning of your selection and hold down the Alt key while you drag your mouse across and down to select a vertical chunk of text. This trick comes in handy if you need to delete numbers along the left side of some text or a column of a tabbed table.

Here are a few more keyboard navigation tips that will save you time.

Shift+F5 = Scrolling through documents is one way to spend a lot of unproductive time. Imagine, for example, that you are working on a long report and you need to copy a couple of non-contiguous paragraphs from the middle of the document to the end and edit them for the conclusion. You end up scrolling back and forth between two places in the document.

Rather than endlessly hunting to return to the right spot, press Shift+F5. Your cursor jumps back to the last location it was in your document. If you need to go back further, keep pressing Shift+F5 to continue to relocate.

Ctrl+F6 = Along the same lines, the Ctrl+F6 keyboard combination is another big time saver. It switches you from one open document to another with no mousing around.

Ctrl + Mouse = Now in Word XP or 2003 you have another highlighting feature. You can highlight areas of text that are not next to each other. The trick is the Ctrl key. To highlight multiple strings of text, hold down the Ctrl key as you click and drag. The previous blocks of text stay highlighted, so you can apply formatting to all the text blocks at once.

In any version of Word, you can repeat your last action with just one keystroke. In fact, you can even choose the command to use. Function key fans can press F4, or you can use Ctrl+Y. Either command repeats the last action.For example, suppose you just merged two cells in a table. Highlight two more cells and press Ctrl+Y to merge them as well. The repeat command is also great for repeating special border or shading formatting to table cells.

Another useful way to use the repeat command is for complex formatting that needs to be applied in a number of different places. For example, suppose you have a bullet list and you need to change the first word of each item to be Bodoni bold italic 18 point. Instead of choosing all those options from the toolbar for every single bullet, highlight the first section of bullet text. Then choose Format|Font and make your changes in the Font dialog box. Now highlight the next text block and press Ctrl+Y (or press F4). You also can use the repeat command to retype the last bit text you typed if you need to duplicate information.

Armed with these few simple commands, you can get your work done more efficiently with less aggravation.

Speed Up With Styles

Styles don't get as much credit as they should. They are the speed demons of the word processing and desktop publishing worlds. A style is just a group of text formatting characteristics that you give a name. For example, suppose you want all the headings of a document to be big and bold, so they stand out.

You might decide to format your headings in 14-point Arial Bold. Rather than applying 14-point Arial Bold on every line you want to be a heading, you click your style named Heading and the text automatically changes to 14-point Arial Bold. When you use styles, you save time and ensure consistency. Every heading looks like every other heading. The time-savings multiply exponentially in complex documents with many elements formatted in a particular way, such as heading levels, bullets, hanging indents, figures, and captions.

In most programs, styles exist in every document, whether you know it or not. For example, in Microsoft Word, when you open a Blank Document, the paragraph mark you see is formatted with the Normal style. Every style is stored in a document template (including the Normal style).

Use built-in styles

Many programs come with built-in styles such as the Normal or Body Text style and styles for common elements such as Headings. Applying a style is easy. You place your cursor in a paragraph, and choose a style from a list of styles. Your text magically changes to whatever formatting was defined in the style.

Create your own styles

Applying styles is okay, but not very creative. Often the built-in styles are boring or just plain ugly. At some point, you'll want to move on and format your text your own way. You can either modify one of the built-in styles or create new styles. For example, to modify one of the built-in styles in Microsoft Word:

Place your cursor in a paragraph that uses the style you want to change.

Choose Format|Style.

Make sure the style you want to change is highlighted in the style list and click Modify.

If you want the style to be saved in the template, click the Add to Template box.

Click on Format and select the option you want to change from the drop-down list. Make the formatting changes.

Click Apply.

Word automatically updates all text formatted with the style.

Important Note: When you save a document, unless you go through the Style dialog and check the Add to Template check box, your new style is only available in that document. It is not saved into the template unless you tell it to in the Style dialog box.

Creating a new style works almost the same way.

To create a new style:

Make sure your cursor is in the paragraph that you want formatted with the new style.

Choose Format|Style. Click New and type a name in the Style box. If you want the style to be saved in the template, be sure to click the Add to Template box.

Word Styling Efficiency

Over the years, people have said that I'm "good" at using Word because I can create and format documents quickly. Although it's true that I do understand some obscure stuff in Word, when it comes to formatting, I take advantage of just one simple formatting technique. I can format Word documents really quickly because whenever I use one of my templates, I make sure I set up the styles to include keyboard shortcuts.

Word has built-in keyboard shortcuts for a lot of the styles you might already be using every day. For example, click your mouse to place your cursor in a paragraph of text (don't highlight anything). Now press Ctrl+Alt+1. Your text is formatted with the Heading 1 style. If you press Ctrl+Alt+2, your text switches to the Heading 2 style. To change it back to Normal text, press Ctrl+Shift+N. If you press Ctrl+Shft+L, the text changes to the List Bullet style.

As you can imagine, once you have these keyboard shortcuts memorized, you can blaze through document formatting. In fact, you can apply styles without even touching the mouse. A style affects the entire paragraph, so after you format one paragraph, you can use the arrow keys to move your cursor down the page. If you're really tricky, you can even use Ctrl+down arrow to jump directly to the next paragraph.

Because I have created many of my own customized templates, I also have quite a few of my own styles set up. To add shortcuts to your own styles, you need to use the Customize feature. Click Tools|Customize and click the Commands tab. Now make sure you select the correct template from the Save changes in drop-down box and click the Keyboard button. Under Categories, scroll down to Styles and click it. You see all your styles listed to the right. Now find the style you want to have a keyboard shortcut. Click to select it and then click in the Press new shortcut key box. Now just type the shortcut key combination you want to assign to the style. The combination appears in the box. If another shortcut already is using that combination it will appear below. If you want to use your shortcut, click the Assign button. When you're done adding keyboard shortcuts, click Close.

Now all your styles can be just as accessible as Word's built-in styles. And you too can be a fast formatting fiend.

Two Cool Style Controls

Two style controls in Word's Style dialog box can save you a lot of time.

Based On: Any style can be based on another style. For example, if your Normal style is set to Times 11 point, another style based on Normal also is set to Times 11 point unless you change it. If you redefine the Normal style, other styles that are based on Normal change too. Be careful with this feature, as the cascade effect can change many styles at once.

Style for Following Paragraph: Style for Following Paragraph is another powerful feature in the Style dialog box. You can set the style that follows the style you are creating or modifying. By default, the following style is generally going to be set to the style you are creating, but you can change it to any other style in your list of styles.

Non-Printing Characters

Sometimes new Microsoft Word users find that they've accidentally turned on non-printing characters. Although you may be tempted to turn off all those "weird symbols" and forget about them forever, in my opinion, leaving certain nonprinting characters turned on makes Word vastly easier to use.

Word calls anything that doesn't appear on your printout a "nonprinting character." Choose Tools|Options and click the

View tab. You see a bunch of little boxes that turn the display of certain items on and off. If you turn on some of these characters, you may find a number of tasks easier.

For example, applying Styles and formatting is much easier if you display Paragraph Marks. Knowing where your paragraphs begin and end is essential to working with Styles in Word. You also can identify "empty paragraphs," which some people tend use to create blank lines between paragraphs. (As an aside, you'll generally have better luck with your formatting if you use the Space Before or After commands instead.)

If you work with tabular text, you should display the tabs as well. I've seen many tables created with 60 tabs when just 2 would have sufficed. People just keep hitting the Tab key in an effort to get the text to line up and get frustrated when it doesn't. If you "show tabs" and adjust your tab settings you can avoid problems because you can actually see what's going on.

Similarly, when you are working with fields, it helps to turn on Hidden Text and Field Codes. For example, if you need to search and replace a term that appears in a book, you must turn on hidden text so the search will find the index entries as well as the text within the document.

Here's another helpful idea for those with slow computers. If you are working with imported graphics, try turning on Picture Placeholders to reduce the amount of time Word spends redrawing the screen. When Picture Placeholders is enabled, Word hides the imported graphics and replaces them with an empty box. You can still see how large your graphic is, but you no longer have to witness the screen redraw process.

I find that the one non-printing character I don't want to turn on is the space character. When the space character is enabled, it is extremely difficult and annoying to try and proofread text on the screen. So you may want to experiment. Exploring the view options may give you a new insight into your document creation experience.

Remove Formatting

One confusing aspect of styles is that any formatting you apply using the formatting commands (i.e. without using styles) can change how your text appears. When you work with styles, it can be difficult to tell whether you applied formatting with a style or using the formatting commands (called "local" formatting). Any local formatting commands you apply override the formatting set up in the style. So sometimes you can end up with text that doesn't look as you expected (such as one piece of text with a Heading 1 style, that doesn't look like every other Heading 1).

To make a document appear visually consistent throughout, it's almost as important to learn how to remove formatting as it is to learn how to apply it. That way, you can take out all the extraneous local formatting and reapply the styles correctly.

In Microsoft Word, to remove all local font formatting, highlight the paragraph and type Ctrl+spacebar. If the spacing has been adjusted manually, it too overrides the spacing set up in the style. To remove this local paragraph spacing formatting, highlight the paragraph and type Ctrl+Q.

If you do a lot of word processing or desktop publishing, spending a little time figuring out how to set up styles can save you a lot of time in the long run.

Changing the Defaults

Many people don't realize that you can open templates just like you open other documents. That includes the default Normal.dot template.

Choose File|Open and change the Files of type drop-down box to Templates (*.dot).

When the template is open, choose Format, Style. Click a style and choose Modify. Be sure that Add to template is checked.

Make any other changes to styles or the template.

Save and close the file. When you save the template, any *new* documents using the Normal template will reflect the changes you made in the Normal.dot file.

If you want your older documents that use the Normal template to reflect the changes you made, you need to open the files and "reattach" your new Normal.dot. Choose Tools, Templates and Add-Ins. Click Attach and choose the template. Then click Open. Again make sure you check the Automatically update document styles check box in the Templates and Add-Ins dialog box. Any styles in the document with the same names as the template styles will be updated with the formatting changes you made to the template styles.

You also can change the default character formatting:

Choose Format|Font.

Choose a font name in the Font box, change the size, or change formats.

When you finish changing the default formatting, click the Default button.

When Word displays a dialog box asking you to confirm that you want to change the default font for the current template, click Yes.

Word immediately makes changes the current document. If Word later asks you to confirm changes when you close the document, choose the Yes button again.

Creating Readable Documents

I confess that ugly, unreadable documents are one of my pet peeves. With word processing software, it is easy to create a nice looking document, so it's sad that many hideous acts of layout continue to be committed. Here are a few tips for creating documents that are a pleasure to read.

1. Use white space effectively.

As the name indicates, white space is any part of the page that does not contain text. If you decide to change the margins of your document, consider the ramifications. Squashing more text on the page by decreasing the margins leads to a document no one wants to read. Margins that are too big are almost as bad, leaving the reader wondering about all the trees that had to die because you wanted to make your document look more "substantial."

2. Watch your line spacing.

White space also includes the spacing in between lines of text. For example, it helps readability to set spacing so headings look like they belong with the text that goes with them. In other words, you need to increase the amount of space above the heading and decrease the amount below it, so the heading and the text it is associated with form a "block." In Word, for example, you change line spacing by choosing Format, Paragraph. In the Spacing section, edit the numbers in the Above and Below fields. Note that your body text (Normal) should have spacing above or below the paragraph, so your eye can easily distinguish where paragraphs begin and end. However, as with margins, if you increase the spacing between lines too much, it looks like you're trying to artificially lengthen the document.

3. Use typefaces appropriately.

Just because you have 700 fonts on your system does not mean you should use them all. Consider the document and use an appropriate typeface. For example, don't use Comic Sans in a professional business document; it just looks stupid. If you think you "might" have used too many fonts, you probably did. From a design standpoint, it's generally more effective to stick with just one or two fonts in a document. As with margins, don't go to extremes. It's rarely a good idea to use enormous or tiny fonts in a business document. Along the same lines, control your use of text emphasis such as like bold and italic, and special formatting like borders, colors, and so forth. Remember the old adage; if you try and emphasize everything, you end up emphasizing nothing.

When you look at professional layouts, you'll notice that the ones that catch your eye don't use every graphic treatment under the sun. Pros know that clean, simple, readable designs are extremely effective. If you take the time to create legible layouts, you'll be rewarded with designs people are actually willing to read.

Tricky Type Techniques

So you've been tasked to create an important document that is supposed to look nice, but you have no illustrations to spice it up. And now you are faced with a boring sea of Times New Roman. Not all of us are blessed with huge clip art libraries or endless funds to purchase stock photography. In certain documents, sometimes the subject matter doesn't lend itself to illustration anyway. So what do you do when you don't have any graphics, but you still want professional-looking, attractive pages? The answer is as close as your font list. Use the type itself to add zest to your page. So the next time you are feeling graphic despair, try out these sample techniques in your word processing or desktop publishing program.

1. **Add Bullets**. The lowly bullet is a quick and easy way break up your pages. By listing items with bullets, you add white space into the page, which breaks it up visually. Most dull documents suffer from a lack of white space (consider an IRS publication, for example). You also don't have to use the plain old filled circle bullet. You can use special characters such as check marks or boxes. Or special picture fonts such as Zapf Dingbats. Adding a bullet is often simple. In Word, you choose Format|Bullets and Numbering to access alternate bullets.

2. **Try an Initial Cap**. Oversized initial capital letters are a decorative type treatment, you often see in books. But there's no reason not to include them in your own documents as well. A raised cap sit on the first line of text, but are much larger than the following text. Conversely, a drop cap spans down below its own line of text. In Word, creating a drop cap is easy, you just choose Format|Drop Cap.

After you have created drop caps, you can format them like any other character. In fact, many times you'll notice that drop caps are formatted in a completely different font. Decorative fonts work well for drop caps because they showcase the beauty of the typeface. Take note of drop cap designs in the printed material and you may find some cool ideas you can borrow.

3. **Create a Pull Quote**. A pull quote is text that has been pulled out of an article and made larger to stand out. Newspapers use this technique a lot to highlight particularly interesting elements of a story. Creating a pull quote is easy. In Word, you create a text box and place it within the surrounding text so the text flows around it.

4. **Add Ruling Lines**. Ruling lines or rules are another easy way to spice up type. A ruling line is just a line that appears above or below a paragraph. They are especially useful for headings or other type that needs to stand out. To add ruling lines in Word, choose Format|Borders and Shading. The line stretches across the entire paragraph. You can change the style, width, color, and shade.

5. **Reverse Out Text**. Sometimes in a long document, it can be striking to create white text on a black background. This technique is called a reverse out. You can create reverse outs in Word by choosing Format|Borders and Shading. In the Shading tab, change the color to black, which also automatically turns the text white. Note that this affects the entire paragraph. You can create similar effect using tables by formatting the cell backgrounds. To create a centered headline, for example, you can create a three-column table and place reversed out text only in the center cell.As with any design treatment, always remember that less is more. An initial cap at the beginning of the page is nice. An initial cap on every paragraph is not. Used in moderation, a few tricky type techniques can help you embellish even the most graphically=challenged documents.

Creating Long Documents in Word

Not too long ago someone asked me how best to create a 400-page manual in Word. She really likes the automatic Table of Contents feature, but after using Word for a 70-page manual, she was worried about how it would cope with a document that was likely to be six times longer.

She was wise to think about this question BEFORE she got started. Many people don't and experience untold levels of frustration as they try to make Word work for long documents. The bad news is that although Word has built-in long document features, the longer the document gets, the more unstable Word becomes.

There are two main rules to follow when creating long documents in Word. One: don't use the Master Documents feature. It hasn't ever worked correctly in any version of Word. So unless you happen to have a perfect installation, the perfect combination of service patches, and a lot of luck, it probably still won't work for you either. My advice is just don't go there.

Second: break your document up into separate files, such as chapters. As I noted, the longer a document gets, the more unstable Word becomes. If you include graphics or tables, you add another level of complexity. The more complex the document, the more unstable it's likely to be as it gets longer. Even if you break your document up into separate chapter files, you can still create a table of contents and index. The trick is to use fields.

In your table of contents or index document file, you use Word's RD (Referenced Document) fields. The RD fields retrieve your chapter files just long enough for Word to compile the table of contents or index.

You can find lots of information about how to use Word fields in the Word help file. Creating long documents in Word is a large topic and there is a page on our Web site that explains it fully. If a long document is in your future, check out http://www.logicalexpressions.com/longdoc.htm for more information.

Use Word's Document Map

We're working on project that involves creating custom forms in Word. Since we like to help educate our clients on this stuff in addition to just doing the work, I ended up passing on a couple of cool Word tips. I figured other folks might like them too.

Our client is working with really large documents (50-100) pages and was complaining that scrolling through pages and pages of text was tedious. So, here's a useful built-in feature. The key is that you need to use Word's built-in heading styles to format your headings (choose Heading 1, Heading 2 and so on from the Styles drop-down). Then if you are using Word 97 or higher, you can jump to any section of the document by choosing View|Document Map. A navigational bar comes up on the side listing all the headings. You just double-click an entry and Word jumps you there.

People who are working on large documents often need to have them reviewed by a number of people. Although you can use Word's revision marks, sometimes you just want to ask a question of the author or the next person in the review cycle. You can add comments anywhere in a document with Word's built-in "comment" feature. Choose Insert|Comment and Word pops out a line with a comment at the end. Type in your text and when you're done, just click back in your document.

Comments can be distracting, so you can make them invisible by choosing View|Markup. To read the comment, you just hover over the yellow text and the comment pops up like a post-it note. To edit the comment, you just show the comments and delete the text and retype it.

Sometimes people want to keep parts of a document from being changed by others. You can use a Word feature called "protecting" a document to prevent modifications. This feature is mostly designed for forms, where you want someone to fill in boxes, but not modify the descriptive text around it. You can either protect an entire document or break the document up into sections and protect just part of it. To insert a section break, choose Insert|Break and choose one of the options under Section. To protect the section, choose Tools|Protect Document. In the Task Pane that appears you can choose to restrict formatting to certain styles or restrict editing completely, limit entry to areas such as form fields, or comments.

Understand Columns and Indents

If you are working on a document like a newsletter that has somewhat complex formatting, you may be wondering how people achieve certain common layout effects in Word. For example, many times in a brochure, you'll find enlarged text formatted differently within lines or a box that has been used for graphic effect. This feature is called a "pull quote," and speaking from experience, it's often used when the designer doesn't have enough text or graphics to fill out the pages, so they're looking for something to make the document more visually interesting.

The way to create a pull quote is by combining Word's Paragraph formatting commands with the border commands. Generally, pull quotes are indented on both sides of the paragraph. To indent the paragraph, highlight it and choose Format|Paragraph. In the Indentation section, type in left and right margins. For example, you might put in .5 to indent the text half an inch from each side. To enclose the text in lines or a box, with the paragraph highlighted, choose Format|Borders and Shading. Choose a Line style and then click in the Preview area to add the lines to the sides of the paragraph you want (above, below, or all the way around).

In brochures or newsletters, you often may want a heading to span columns. Many people know how to create columns, but it's a little trickier to have columns mixed in with text that spans them. However, it's easy once you know the trick. First, create your columns as you normally would, by choosing Format|Columns. Make sure that the Apply to drop-down says Whole Document. (Don't worry that the heading will end up in a column.)

Now select just the heading paragraph that you want to span columns, and choose Format|Columns again. Click the columns button, and select 1 column. Note that the Apply to drop-down says "Selected Text." That means your column setting will only apply to the heading.

To change columns in the middle of a document, Word needs to put in Continuous Section Breaks. This process is sort of a pain to do manually using the Insert|Break command, but by highlighting the heading and changing the columns, Word adds the necessary Section Breaks for you. If you decide to delete the breaks later, the easiest way to see them is to switch to Normal view by choosing View|Normal. Section breaks appear as double lines with the words Section Break (Continuous) in the middle. If you delete the Section Breaks, the column formatting stored in them goes away.

Word Weirdness

As someone who moved over to Word from Word Perfect many years ago, I can sympathize with the pain of changing word processors. The transition was ugly, but I wasn't alone. Over the years, many people have migrated from Word Perfect to Word. In response to the large number of new users, Microsoft added a couple of options designed to help these new users get acquainted with the World of Word.

Unfortunately, these options have caused more trouble than they are worth. If the Word Perfect options are turned on, weirdness results. For example, new Word users may wonder why when they select a block of text and press the Delete key, nothing happens. Delete should mean delete, after all.

However, if you check the status bar at the bottom of the screen, you'll notice that it says, "Delete Block? No (Yes)." The idea is that if you press Y to confirm the delete, the text goes away, just like the old days of Word Perfect. But most people when they press the Delete key have already made the command decision to delete text now, so the extra step is overkill.

To make Word behave better, you need to remove the option settings that relate to Word Perfect. Choose Tools|Options and click the General tab. You'll notice two options at the bottom of the list regarding Word Perfect. Remove the checkmark from both check boxes and click OK. You will be rewarded with an absence of delete confirmation messages.

When the Word Blank Document Isn't Blank

Recently, I got a question from a reader who was distressed because when he went to create a new document in Word, the Blank Document wasn't blank. Somehow, he'd managed to add text into his Blank Document, so he was forced to delete out a bunch of stuff before he could do anything in Word.

Every document in Word is based on a template. In general, creating a new template is easy. You just create a document and then Choose File|Save As and change the Save as type to Document Template (*.dot). The Blank Document you get by default when you create a new document in Word is actually based on a template called Normal.dot. If you accidentally get text in there, you need to open the Normal.dot template, remove the text, and resave the file. Word won't let you save a regular document as the Normal.dot template (you get an unhelpful error message). So you have to open Normal.dot directly and resave it.

Probably the hardest thing is figuring out where the Normal. dot template is on your computer. Later versions of Word put it deep in a folder hierarchy based on your username, so it's something like: C:\Documents and settings \Your Name\ Application Data\Microsoft\Templates. You can find out where it is stored by choosing Tools|Options|File Locations and looking at User Templates. Alternatively, you can do a search in Windows Explorer for Normal.dot. Once you find the file, either right-click it in Windows Explorer and choose Open or from within Word, choose File|Open. Whatever you do, don't double-click the filename. That just causes a new document to be created that's based on the Normal template. Once you have found and opened the Normal.dot file, remove the text and save it.

Unfortunately, it is possible for things to go really wrong with a template, so it becomes corrupted. If so, it's better to just start over. If Word can't find the Normal.dot template when it opens, it has to regenerate a fresh one. Any custom settings in your old Normal.dot such as formatting, macros or AutoText will be lost and you'll be back to the plain-vanilla version that comes with Word. If you love your custom settings, you can rename your old Normal.dot to Normal-old.dot and then let Word generate a new Normal template. Then you can choose Tools|Templates and Add-ins and click the Organizer button. In the Template Organizer, you can then pull in stuff you want from your old Normal.dot.

Troubleshooting Word

Recently, I ran into a problem where Word would crash immediately upon opening. It would flash up the standard screen and then just sit there frozen. I'd have to end the program to make it go away. To end a non-responsive program, you press Ctrl+Alt+Del and in the Applications tab, highlight the offending program and click End Process. Usually the offending program will say Not Responding in the Status column. (With my Word situation, I had pretty much figured that out.)

In any case, because the problem was new, I figured that some software I had installed recently caused Word to die. Realistically, I use Word almost every day, so I didn't have to search too far back in my memory banks to determine the software I'd installed. I had loaded a trial of Stamps.com software the day before.

It took me a while to figure out the relationship actually. As it turned out, I had selected an optional Word addressing feature, since it seemed like a nice idea. However, crashing Word was unacceptable, so it had to go. The question was how to get it out of Word.

To include extra features from outside vendors, Word uses a concept called an "add-in." These additional programs or templates are loaded when you start Word. If Word is crashing on start-up, a wayward add-in is often to blame. You can tell if that's the problem by starting Word with no add-ins. If it runs and doesn't crash, you can be pretty sure the add-in is to blame. That's what happened in my case with the Stamps.com software.

To run Word with no add-ins, you need to use the /a switch. Click Start, Run and click the Browse button to find Winword. exe (the folder depends on which version you are using). Type a space after the path, then add /a.

To get rid of the Add in, I had to play a little game. First I put the COM Add-ins button on the toolbar, so I could find the Stamps.com add-in. Choose Tools|Customize and in the commands tab, click the Tools category and drag the COM Add-ins button to the toolbar. When you click the button, you see the Add-ins that are available. I then clicked Remove to ditch the Stamps.com one. From that, I was able to determine the file name and since I was annoyed, I also rummaged around my hard disk and deleted the add-in file itself too, just to be really sure it wouldn't come back.

Fix Word Line Break Problems

When you paste text into Word sometimes you can end up with odd line breaks. This problem often happens when you are copying and pasting from an email, for example. Instead of coming in as a complete line like this:

"The quick brown fox jumped over the lazy dog's back."

The text is broken up like this:

"The quick brown fox

jumped over the lazy

dog's back."

In other words, although the margins may be set to stretch across the page, the text does not. Many people will laboriously fix the problem line by line, but it's a tedious process.

The problem has to do with extra line breaks, not the margins. In some cases, you can use Word's Autoformat to reformat the lines. Highlight the text and choose Format|Autoformat. However, depending on where the text was copied from, this approach doesn't always work.

If you turn on paragraph markers, you can tell what is causing the text to break. Choose Tools|Options and in the View tab, click Paragraphs and Tabs. If the lines have line breaks at the end of each line, you'll see little left pointed arrows. If they are paragraph breaks, you'll see the pilcrow character, which looks like a backwards P.

To get rid of the breaks, you can do a find and replace. If the markers are showing line breaks at the end of each line, you can find them by putting ^l (a lowercase letter L) in the Find What box. If they are paragraph markers, put ^p in the Find What box.

In the Replace box, simply type a space and then click Find Next. As you go through the document, you will remove the unwanted breaks. The text will span the entire width of the page.

Sharing Word Files Successfully

I was talking to a colleague who was struggling with a Word document that looked different, depending on where it was opened. She wanted her client to be able to edit the documents later, but the same document that looked great on her computer looked awful on the client's computer.

The main problem with sharing Word files is that Word gets a lot of information from the computer it is running on. Part of how Word makes the document look more or less like it will look when printed (aka What You See is What You Get or WYSIWYG) depends a lot on the printer that is selected and the fonts loaded on the computer.

However, you can do a few things to help make sure your Word file looks as you intended on another computer. If you know the files will be used elsewhere, find out what printer they use and then select that printer, even if it's not attached to your computer. You can install a printer in Windows, even if you don't physically have the machine. (Do a search in the Windows help for "printer drivers" for more information.)

The other thing you can do is stick to using the somewhat generic fonts that are available on all Windows systems. For example, every Windows computer has Times New Roman and Arial installed. Yes, they are boring, but they have been used in every version of Windows, so unless someone has done something really weird to their system, those fonts should be available.

Finally, avoid using hard page breaks in your document (i.e. pressing Ctrl+Enter) or adding a whole bunch of carriage returns to force text down to a new page. Instead, use some of the paragraph formatting commands such as "Keep with next" or "Keep lines together" to keep the text you want to stay together on the same page. Just highlight the text and choose Format|Paragraph, and in the Line and Page Break tab, you'll find these commands. Another handy one for important breaks such as section or chapter headings is "Page break before." This command is great when you want to make sure a heading starts on a new page.

These tips don't necessarily guarantee your document will look the same on another computer, but they're a good start. What you lose in creativity, you gain in compatibility.

Remove Word Hyperlinks

Newer versions of Microsoft Word are Internet-aware. When you type in a Web site address or e-mail address by default, Word turns this Internet-related text into a hyperlink so you can automatically launch your browser or e-mail program. This type of auto-feature is rarely useful to me and most of the time just drives me nuts. Many times, I want a hyperlink to be just plain, old boring text. In other words, I don't want the blue or underlining, and I'm never going to click it. (Plus, if you import Word files into a desktop publishing program, you know that extra formatting can cause problems!)

So the question is, how do you make Word stop autoformatting hyperlinks? The procedure is slightly different in Word 2000 and Word XP, but in both cases, you need to change options in two places. In Word 2000, choose Tools|AutoCorrect. (In Word XP, you choose Tools|AutoCorrect Options instead.) In the Autoformat as you Type tab, click to remove the checkmark next to Internet and network paths with hyperlinks.

Now click the AutoFormat tab. Click to remove the checkmark next to Internet and network paths with hyperlinks.

Now Word won't automatically format your hyperlinks and e-mail addresses. That's a huge relief for some of us, but the change only affects new documents. It doesn't fix hyperlinks that are already in your document.

Making a hyperlink or e-mail address plain, old text means you have to tell Word that you don't want it to be a field. To change the hyperlink, highlight it and press Ctrl+Shift+F9 to unlink the field. (Yes, you use the F9 function key on the top row of your keyboard.) The hyperlink turns to plain text. If there is still unwanted extra formatting, press Ctrl+spacebar to remove it.

Mysterious Word Behavior

Not too long ago, I put together a newsletter in Word. I combined six documents that I received from other people and formatted them consistently into the newsletter. The process made me think about how Word users often are completely mystified when Word seems to change the formatting of text pasted in from other places.

The thing that most people don't realize is that in Word, there are two distinct ways to format text: using styles or using "local formatting." Local formatting is text changes you've applied to a paragraph using the commands in the Format menu or toolbar buttons. You format a paragraph with a style when you select a name from the Style toolbar button.

People always say, "oh I don't use styles." The reality is that yes, you do. Whether you realize it or not, every single paragraph in every single document has a style. That style is called Normal. You may have added 25 font changes to every paragraph in the document, but to Word, underneath, all that text is still using that Normal style.

So when you copy text in from another document, Word is looking at the style. Suppose you copy in a passage of text from a document that has its Normal style set to Arial 10 point. You copy that text into your document where the Normal style is formatted as Times New Roman. When you paste your text, it takes on the formatting of Normal style in the receiving document. If the Normal style is Times New Roman, that's how your text appears.

Okay, so that's what happens if there is no local formatting. However, when text is copied from one document to another, it retains local formatting. So if you made one piece of text blue in the middle of a paragraph by choosing Format|Font, that text will still be blue when you copy it. The text around it will change to the formatting of the Normal style in the receiving document.

Understanding what's going on can work to your advantage. For example, in my newsletter, none of the 6 documents I combined had any special styles or local formatting defined. So I was able to choose Insert|File and add the files into the newsletter. The files took on the formatting of the Normal style I had defined in the newsletter automatically. I didn't have to change any formatting at all.

Another way to avoid formatting problems is to dump formatting completely and start over. In that case, you can copy text and then in the receiving document, choose Edit|Paste Special. Then choose the Unformatted text option and you'll get only the text with no local formatting at all.

Get Pictures Out of Word

For years, desktop publishers have asked their clients to save their pictures and their images as separate files. For example, if you're a freelance writer, you may have noticed that most magazines always tell writers to submit photographs or other images separately from their articles. There's a reason for that. Desktop publishing software needs to have words and images as separate files so they can be assembled into a layout, such as a magazine page. DTP software can't import complex Word files correctly, so a lot of author formatting goes away. (I've often thought about how much time is wasted by authors trying to "pretty up" their files.)

Of course, I've been an editor for many years, so I have spent more than my fair share of time attempting to extract pictures out of Word files from those people who did not follow the instructions. It can be a huge pain to get graphics back out after they've been pasted into Word. Many times the image quality suffers, but sometimes if you are lucky, you can extract them.

Depending on the type of graphic file and how the writer embedded the files in Word in the first place, sometimes it's relatively easy to just select the picture and press Ctrl+C to copy it to the clipboard. Then you can paste the image into a graphic program and save the file separately.

Another thing that sometimes works is pasting the file into PowerPoint. Then you can right-click and choose Save as picture. The resulting file's resolution is dependent on the original file's resolution when it was embedded in Word, not on its scaled size. So sometimes you can get a better quality file that way, especially if the original was a vector line art image (as opposed to a bitmap).

If the pictures are screen captures or other low-resolution bitmaps, one sneaky way to get around the problem is to try saving the file as HTML. Choose File, Save As and change the Save As Type drop down to Web page (*.htm, *.html). When you do the save as, Word creates GIF or JPG files of all the graphics. Although the image quality is only screen resolution, this method is by far, the fastest way I've found of saving graphics as files when they've been embedded in a Word doc. If you have a manual with 200 screen captures that need to be extracted, it's certainly worth a try.

Font Fun

Like most people, I have a lot of fonts on my system. Selecting which font to use and making sure other people see those fonts can be a challenge. But you can get around both problems and have font happiness.

Windows has a feature that lets you look at fonts by similarity, which makes it easier to select just the right font for your project. Go into Windows Explorer and navigate to C:\ windows\fonts. You'll see all your fonts listed. At the top of the window, you also see a number of buttons. Click the one that has AB on it to list fonts by similarity or choose the option from the View menu. After you do, you'll see a drop-down box called "List fonts by similarity to:". Click the drop-down to select a font and the fonts below re-sort with a notation as to how similar they are to the selected font. Unfortunately, this technique doesn't necessarily work with all fonts. Some of the fonts loaded on my system ended up relegated to the bottom with a notation that says No Panose Information available. Panose is a font matching system, so the message means Windows could figure out whether the font is similar or not.

Many Word users have encountered font problems when they open a document on another system. By default, unless both computers have the exact same fonts loaded, Windows will substitute fonts. This situation can cause great consternation as your perfectly crafted formatting goes down the drain.

The good news is that you can get around the problem by embedding the fonts into your Word document. The bad news is that it only works with True Type fonts and it can dramatically increase the file size. To embed the fonts in a document choose Tools|Options and click the Save tab. Then add a check mark next to Embed True Type fonts.

You also can optionally choose to embed only the characters you used in the document, which can reduce the file size somewhat. To do that in the Options dialog box, place a checkmark next to Embed characters in use only. Another option is to click Do not embed common system fonts, which tells Word to avoid embedding common fonts such as Arial and Times New Roman that are on almost all Windows machines.

Dealing with Overtype Mode

Imagine you're merrily editing a document in Word and then suddenly, much to your dismay you realize that at some point you pressed the Insert key and you just typed over a whole bunch of text. You might be able to Undo it by pressing Ctrl+Z, but it's still really annoying.

Word can type in two modes: Insert mode and Overtype mode. In the Status Bar at the bottom of your screen, you'll notice that OVR is generally grayed out. That means you are in Insert mode. When your cursor is placed in the text and you type, the new text you type is inserted in between the text that was there before. If you press the Insert key on your keyboard, you see OVR in your status bar, and the text you type erases whatever was there before, instead of pushing it over.

Obviously, when you discover that you've inadvertently entered Overtype mode, the first thing to do is press the Insert key to go back into Insert mode. Then you have to fix whatever text you just destroyed. If you don't want to deal with this problem again, you have a number of workarounds.

One creative workaround I read about, but have never used, is to put something on the Insert key itself, such as a Band-aid or tape to make the key harder to press. Plus, it will feel odd, so you are less likely to accidentally press it.

Another way to deal with Word is to click the option to use Insert for pasting text, instead of switching into Overtype mode. Choose Tools|Options and click the Edit tab. Click to add a checkmark next to Use the INS key for paste. Then when you accidentally hit Insert, you get a bunch of pasted text, which might be easier to clean up than the mess you can make in Overtype mode.

Unless you want to create a macro, a better alternative is to assign the Insert key to something useful and easy to ignore if necessary. For example, if you go into the Format Font dialog box a lot, it actually could be useful to use the Insert key bring it up. And if you press it accidentally, all you'll see is a dialog box, which you can close.

To remap the key, choose Tools|Customize and click the Keyboard button. Under Categories, click All Commands. Now scroll down and find FormatFont. Put your cursor in the Press new Shortcut key box and press the Insert key. Then click the Assign button. Now when you press Insert, you get the Format Font dialog box in your face instead of accidentally overtyping a bunch of text.

Page Numbering in Word

Most people know how to add page numbers at the bottom of their documents. You just go into Header and Footer view, click the little number icon and voila, the page number prints on every page. But fewer folks know that you also can add snazzier page numbers almost as easily. For example, you can put "Page 1 of 24" at the bottom of the document. As your document gets longer, Word automatically increases the number.

How you add this information varies slightly, depending on your version of Word. When you switch to Header and Footer view, you see the Header and Footer toolbar. Older versions of Word have slightly different buttons. In Word 97 or 2000, type the word "Page" and a space in your header or footer and then click the Insert Page Number button. Now type another space, the word "of" and a space. In the Header and Footer toolbar, click the Insert Number of Pages button.

Older versions of Word don't have the Insert Number of Pages button, but you can still add the number of pages. Just choose Insert|Field and select NumPages. Here's another little twist on the problem for Word 2000 users. If you have the first release of Word 2000, the NumPages field is broken. Everything looks okay on the screen, but instead of printing out "Page 1 of 24" it prints "Page 1 of 1," "2 of 2," and so on. This problem can be frustrating, but there are a couple of workarounds.

The first (and easiest) workaround is to upgrade Word 2000 to the latest Service Release, which is a good idea anyway. You can find downloadable Service Releases on Microsoft's Web site (www.microsoft.com) or you can usually get them on CD as well. If you just have to get the document done right now, you also can cheat. First, insert a bookmark at the end of your document (choose Insert|Bookmark). Then, where you would have used the NumPages field, insert a PageRef field that references the bookmark at the end of the document instead. The trick is to make sure that if you add more text later, you keep the bookmark at the end of the document.

Dealing with Header and Footer Weirdness

Many Word users dread creating long documents with multiple sections because you need to get deeply involved in making headers and footers work. Let's face it, the way Word deals with headers and footers is a pain. To get to your headers and footers, you can either choose View|Header and Footer, or double click an existing header or footer in the grayed out area in Print Layout view.

Either way, your header and footer becomes editable and you see the Header and Footer toolbar. That's where the fun starts. Suppose for example, that you have a document where you want to have each new chapter name display in the header. If you move the chapters around or edit the text, your headers may go nuts.

Most of the aggravation surrounding headers and footers stems from one button: the Same As Previous button in the Header and Footer toolbar. This feature is a convenience if you want all your headers and footers to look the same. (Then again, if you are creating multiple sections in a document, you probably don't want the section headers and footers to look the same - that might be why you created sections in the first place.) The idea is that you use the Same as Previous button to tell Word to copy the header from the previous section into the current one.

The concept sounds nice, but it can drive you crazy when header information is copied to sections where you don't want it. It's sort of a creepy ripple effect, and if it's happened to you, I'm sure you k now what I mean. My advice to keep yourself from losing your mind is to make sure that when you edit headers and footers always break the Same as Previous link for each section. As you click the Show Next or Show Previous buttons to go through the headers or footers, your goal is to see no little "Same as Previous" text on the right hand side above the dotted rectangle surrounding the header or footer.

After you've broken the links, it's easy to just copy the information that is the same from one header to the next and edit it. Remember, your goal is to make sure that the Same As Previous button is never activated (it looks sort of pushed in or grayed out when it's deactivated). If you already have text in the header or footer, and a lot of sections, deactivating the Same As Previous button can cause unexpected things to happen. After you unlink every section, you can copy what you want into the header or footer without anything automatic messing up your document.

Add a Filename in a Word Footer

A reader wrote in with the following question:

"My question is that when I see text documents from others, I see a file location reference in the lower left corner of the document. I use Microsoft Word 2000. Is there a way to get the file location to automatically print in that, or other footer location? I have tried help screens but have not hit the right subject, I guess."

I thought this question was a good one and might be useful for a lot of other people. Especially for those who tend to forget where they put their files. If you include the full path in the document, you can't lose track of the file. (Unless, of course, you lose the print out too -- I can't help with that.)

To add the file location, in Word you need to use a field. You can put it anywhere in the document. Because the question specifically mentions including it in the footer, the following steps explain how to put it there:

1. Choose View|Header and Footer

2. Click the Switch Between Header and Footer button on the Header and Footer toolbar to switch to the footer.

3. Once your cursor is sitting in the footer, choose Insert|Field.

4. Under Categories, click Document Information.

5. Under FieldName, choose FileName.

6. To add the full path, click Add path to filename under Options button.

7. Click OK.

And voila, your filename and path appears in the footer of every page. Click Close to exit Header and Footer view and return to the document.

Another Way to Add Footer Information

After reading my tip about adding file path information into a Word footer, an astute reader pointed out another method of inserting the information. His technique works in Word 97 and later. My approach was to just add a field manually using the Insert|Field command. If you hate the idea of fields, you can shield yourself from that technology by using the Insert Auto Text button instead. To add the pathname this way, follow these steps.

1. Choose View|Header and Footer

2. Click the Switch Between Header and Footer button on the Header and Footer toolbar to switch to the footer.

3. Once your cursor is sitting in the footer, click the "Insert AutoText" button on the Header and Footer toolbar. A pop-up menu appears with a number of choices, including "File name and path."

4. After you choose it from the list, the filename appears in the footer.

You also can choose to add other information such as the author name or "page X of Y" automatically. However, in this situation it helps to understand what Word is actually doing. I've talked about AutoText in this column before. Basically, it lets you save a block of text with a name. That text can include fields. So when you are inserting the "canned" text using the

Insert AutoText button, behind the scenes, Word is still using fields. And as I discussed in another column the NumPages field is broken in certain versions of Word 2000. So the AutoText based on that field is equally broken.

So in certain versions of Word 2000, because of the broken field, when you print your pages, instead of getting "page x of y" Word prints 1 of 1, 2 of 2, 3 of 3 and so on. You can download the fix from Microsoft.

Tabs in Microsoft Word

A reader was frustrated trying to get Microsoft Word to set tabs correctly in her documents. Here are a few tips I gave her, which might help a few other long-suffering Word users too.

The first thing to do when you work with tabs is to show the ruler (choose View and make sure there's a checkmark next to Ruler). Then you'll see the little icons in the ruler when you click in a line of text. The default tabs are the little vertical dashes that appear in the gray area below the numbers on the ruler (at .5 inch increments).

If you click in the ruler, you set a tab. For example, a left tab looks like a little "L" in the white area. To get rid of a tab you set, you just click and drag it off the ruler. You can also set tabs more precisely and/or change the default tab settings by choosing Format|Tabs. Note that the tabs affect only the paragraph you are in, so if you want to change the tabs for an entire document, you need to choose Edit|Select All (or press Ctrl+A) to select the entire document first. (Note that if you use Word's styles, you can set tabs for all paragraphs using a particular style as well.)

Indents and hanging indents are modified with the little triangles on the left-hand side of the ruler. If you want to create an indent, you drag the top upside-down triangle to the right. To create a hanging indent (for example, to change the distance a bullet is from text) you drag the bottom triangle. (Again, you need to pay attention to where your cursor is...the change will only affect the paragraph you are in unless you highlight the other text you want changed.)

If you are doing something complicated with tabs it can help to "show tabs." Choose Tools|Options and click the View tab. Place a checkmark next to Tab Characters in the Formatting marks section. Then you'll see little arrows that indicate where you have a tab. For really complicated stuff, it's sometimes actually easier to create a table with no borders. One quickie thing you can do for a complicated group of tabbed items is type them all in with just ONE tab in between the entry. Then when you are done entering text, highlight it and choose Table|Convert Text to Table.

Tab Dos and Don'ts

In the last tip, I talk about tabbed text. Now I'd like to talk about when you don't want to use tabs. For example, if you are one of those people who like to put a tab at the beginning of each paragraph to indent it, please don't. There is a better way. Instead, use Word's first line indent setting. You can find this setting by highlighting the paragraph and choosing Format|Paragraph. Under Special change the drop down to First line and next to By use the up and down arrows to set a measurement. Click OK and you never have to tab again.

If you have two paragraphs of text that you want to appear next to each other, you have yet another opportunity to use tabs badly. In this case, I suggest you not use tabs to move the text over into the second column. If you do, you make a large mess if you ever want to edit the text again later. Tabbed text doesn't word wrap. So you should use a table instead. The text wraps within each table cell, so you can edit it later without pain. Many people don't use tables because they think that they are either too difficult or that they always have to have borders. Neither is true.

To add a table, choose Table|Insert|Table. Select the number of rows and columns you want. In this case, if you want two columns of text, you'd set up a three-column table, so you have "spacer" cell in the middle. When the table appears, type text in the left and right columns.

You can turn off borders by choosing Table|Select|Table to highlight the entire table. Then choose Format|Borders and Shading and click None. Once you have learned how to set up tables with invisible borders, you'll probably think of all kinds of ways you can use them. Any time you are wondering how you can make blocks of text line up, consider experimenting with a borderless table. It might be a lot easier than some of the alternatives.

The Many Faces of Tabs

Recently I received the following question:

"We are grappling with how to generate a dot leader in Word. For example we use this all the time:

MARKET VALUE............................$1,525,000

I now copy this from a Word Perfect document that has been converted and I type in the dots manually. Is there a better way?"

The short answer is yes. You can create dot leaders easily if you learn a little about setting tabs. As someone who has spent a lot of time cleaning up bad tabs, I've learned that you can do two things to make your tabular life better. First, know that Word is not a typewriter, so you only need to press the Tab key once in your text if you set it up right. If you show non-printing characters (click the Show/Hide toolbar button that looks like a paragraph) you can tell how many tabs are in each line.

So now you're thinking, okay with just one tab, how do I get my text over far enough? That brings me to my second suggestion: set tabs. Highlight the text you have typed (which, of course, has just one tab in between each item). You then can set tabs by clicking on the ruler or using the menu option. However, to include a dot leader, you need to use the menu, so choose Format|Tabs. In the dialog box, you'll see you have many choices.

Click the type of tab (left, right, center, decimal, bar). Then select the dot leader (option 2) and type the location of the tab. In this case, since the tabbed text involves numbers, you'd probably choose a decimal tab with a dot leader. Click OK and you'll see your new tab stop on the ruler and the text jumps to that location. If it's in the wrong place, just click and drag the tab stop. To remove the tab, you can either click and drag the tab stop off the ruler, or choose Format|Tabs again, select the tab setting, and click the Clear button.

More on Tables

I've written before about how you can create tables with no borders when you need to line up text. Another use for tables is for working with data. Behind the scenes, Word's mail merge feature has used tables for the data for years. Newer versions tend to hide this fact, but basically, when you are merging data into a document, it's probably coming from something in tabular format, whether it's a spreadsheet, database, or other data file.

Sometimes you have to work with data that was not created in Word such as data from an old contact management program, for example. You probably can find some type of export that will let you get the data out into a text or comma-delimited format. The easiest way to deal with the data after you get it into Word is to turn it into a table.

So, once you have your text file exported, select all of it and paste it into a blank Word document. Once it is in Word, take a look at what you've got. In our contact management example, you might have lines of data that began with first name and last name like this:

John   Smith

In this case, your job would be to replace the multiple spaces with tabs and then convert the whole thing into a table. So, first you want to use Find and Replace to replace spaces with tabs. So first figure out how many spaces are between each piece of data (for example, there are 5 spaces between John and Smith). Then choose Edit|Replace.

In the Find what box, type the space bar five times. In the Replace with box type ^t. Then click Replace All. Word replaces every five spaces with one tab.

Now select the all the text by pressing Ctrl+A and choose Table|Convert|Text to Table. In the dialog box, you should see that Word suggests two columns and that text should be separated at Tabs. Click OK and magically a two-column table appears ready for use in a mail merge.

Sorting Text in Word

Many people don't realize that you can sort lists in Word. For example, suppose you plan to send out a bunch of cards to your friends. You might have typed up their names into a document like:

John Smith

Zeke Jones

Charles Green

If you look at the list, you'll notice that they are not in alphabetical order and there's a space in between the first name and the last name. To sort them, highlight the lines of text and choose Table|Sort. In the Sort Text dialog box, it shows that it will sort by paragraphs. Click Okay and you get:

Charles Green

John Smith

Zeke Jones

Now you realize, oops Word sorted the list by the first name. What if you want them sorted by last name? In the Sort Text dialog, click the Options button. Change the radio button to Other and type a space in the box. Click OK. Now change the Sort by drop down to Word 2 and click OK. You now have:

Charles Green

Zeke Jones

John Smith

Another way to accomplish the same thing is to convert the text to a table using the space as a separator between the columns. Then sort by the second column. To convert it, choose Table|Convert|Text to Table. Next to Other add a space. Of course, when sorting, the way the data is set up is important. All the first names need to be one word. If Mary Jo is a first name, you may need to separate Mary and Jo with a non-breaking space (Ctrl+Shift+spacebar), so they stay together.

Keep Word Tables the Same Across Documents

A reader wanted to copy a Word table from one document to another, but when he did, the column spacing changed. So he wanted to know what he needed to do to keep tables from reformatting during a copy and paste.

You can do a number of things to keep tables consistent across documents. First, set the table so it's a fixed width in the Table Properties. The command is mildly different in the various versions of Word, but in Word 2003, you choose Table|Table Properties for example. In the Table Properties dialog box you find a check box for Preferred Width. By default, this setting is generally not checked, so click to add a checkmark next to it and set the size you want your table to be.

Another thing you may want to consider is the use of styles. If you copy and paste a table between two documents that do not use styles, all the text is set to the Normal style. In the new document, the font may change and cause the table to expand and resize to fit the content. Resizing the table to fit the content is another optional setting that's on by default. Back in the Table Properties dialog box, click the Options button and you'll see a check mark text to it. You want to remove that checkmark to keep the table from resizing.

Of course, if you have wildly different font settings in the two documents, you may run into problems. The best way to keep tables consistent across documents is to use the same styles for the text and to set the table width options.

Calculate in Word

It's well documented that I'm not a huge fan of spreadsheets. If I can use Word instead of Excel, I usually do. Of course, I've met people who have the opposite opinion and create vast lists of text in Excel that I would never, ever create. I just think it's a whole lot easier to deal with Word tables than a whole huge spreadsheet.

The good news for people like me is that even though Word doesn't have the calculating power of Excel, you can use it for basic math functions. Since basic math is just about all this human is capable of, I often find Word's calculating feature is all I need to include simple numeric data in my documents. For example, in one of the business plans I wrote, I was able to use Word tables and calculate a simple balance sheet and sales forecast.

Tables like these don't require anything more than addition, and Word is capable of adding the numbers in a column or row together for you. (The commands even look like they do in Excel, if it makes you feel better.) To add the numbers in a row, make sure you've entered all the data, except for the last cell where the result will be placed (generally the right-most cell). Then choose Table|Formula and you'll see that it says =SUM(LEFT), which means "add all the numbers up to the left of the cell." After you click OK, you see that Word has magically put a number into the cell.

Adding a column of numbers works basically the same way. Enter all the data into your column except the last one at the bottom. Click that cell and choose Table|Formula. This time it says =SUM(ABOVE), which means "add up all the numbers above this cell."

If you are really ambitious, you can even enter your own simple calculations using standard Excel-like nomenclature. Even though the cell headings aren't visible like they are in Excel, columns are letters and rows are numbers, so the first cell is A1. If you wanted to multiply your first cell with the second cell in a row you could type in =A1*B1 and Word tells you the answer.

One thing that can be confusing is that the calculations don't necessarily update automatically. To update them, click the cell and press the F9 key. If you have more than one table to update, you can select the whole document by pressing Ctrl+A and then pressing F9.

Use Word's AutoCorrect Effectively

AutoCorrect is one of Word's under-used features. When it's turned on, AutoCorrect automatically fixes common typing mistakes, such as "teh" for "the." It sounds like a good idea, but some people find that level of interruption distressing. If you hate "auto" anything, you may want to turn it off. Choose Tools|AutoCorrect and deselect Replace Text as You Type.

However, what a lot of people don't realize is that you can add more entries to AutoCorrect in addition to the ones that come built into Word. Choose Tools|AutoCorrect. You see a big list of words with the incorrect spellings of the words on the left and the correct spellings on the right. Type the incorrect and correct spelling of a word into the Replace and With boxes. Be sure that Replace Text as You Type is enabled.

Another way to use AutoCorrect is to expand long words or abbreviations. For example, if you work for a business with a convoluted name, such as Johnson, Jackson, Jones and Jacobson, you could create an AutoCorrect entry called "jj" that magically changes this acronym into the full company name.

However, when you add AutoCorrect entries, be sure you don't add an abbreviation that is actually a word. For example, if your company name is Beyond Entertainment, and you create an AutoCorrect entry called "be," you will find the words Beyond Entertainment in a lot more places than you expected.

You can use AutoCorrect to store both text and formatting as well. Highlight some text and choose Tools|AutoCorrect. The highlighted text is inserted into the With box. This way, you can store formatted text such as fields, symbols, paragraph marks, imported graphics, or other non-text objects. Be sure to click the Formatted Text radio button to tell Word to save the entry with its original formatting.

Try Out AutoText in Word

AutoText is the cousin to AutoCorrect. Although AutoText isn't quite as speedy to use, it has a couple of aspects that can make it more flexible in certain situations.

The most important difference between AutoCorrect and AutoText is that you can save AutoText entries with a particular template. AutoCorrect entries are always saved into the Normal.dot template, but with AutoText, you can save the entries to a specific template or copy them between templates.

AutoText also doesn't replace every instance of a certain set keystrokes with a block of text. You must hit the F3 key to activate an AutoText entry. For example, if you create an AutoText entry called "be" for Beyond Entertainment, it wouldn't be replaced every time you type the word be. You have to press F3 to change be to Beyond Entertainment.

To create an AutoText entry:

1. Select the text or graphics you want to store as AutoText. If you want to include formatting in the entry, make sure you include the paragraph mark in your selection.

2. Choose Insert|AutoText|Autotext.

3. In the Enter AutoText entries here box, type a name for the entry. Word suggests a name, but you can type over the selection. If you want the entry to be attached to a specific template, change the Look in drop-down box to a different template. (The default setting is "All active templates.")

4. Click the Add button.

Now when you type your AutoText entry name (such as be) into your document and press F3, your full text appears.

Remove Misspelled Words from the Dictionary

Here's a tip I read about ages ago and promptly forgot. But it's a good one because I know I'm not the only person who has accidentally added a misspelled word to the Microsoft Word dictionary. It's really easy to do.

You probably run the spelling checker all the time. (If not, you should.) Anyway, you run a spell check by choosing Tools|Spelling and Grammar or by pressing the F7 key. So you merrily let Word go through your document and one time instead of pressing Ignore on a weird word, you click Add. Now every time the spell checker encounters that word, instead of marking it as suspect, it flies right by it because you told Word it's correct.

If you have Word set to do spell checking as you type (a.k.a. the squiggly red underlines) it's even easier to add words accidentally. You just right click and with a slip of the mouse, you've added instead of ignored a word.

In any case, adding misspelled words to the dictionary counts as one of those "oops" moments when you wish you could turn back time. But it's not set in stone. You can edit the dictionary and take out your bad words (so to speak).

Choose Tools|Options and click the Spelling and Grammar tab. Now click the Custom Dictionaries button. You see a list of Custom Dictionaries with the one you're using selected. (Most people just have one.) Now click Modify. A window opens with a list of all the words in the dictionary. This page is just a text file that you can edit. Highlight the problem word, press the Delete button to remove it, and clik OK. Then choose

File|Close, and when Word asks you if you want to save the file, click Yes.

While you're editing the file, you also can add words. So if you know you're going to have a document with a lot of odd words, you can just add them into the dictionary text file directly, instead of adding them during a spell check. Just type in one word per line and save the file.

Handy Search and Replace in Word

Although Microsoft Word is reasonably smart about reading HTML and other formatting codes, sometimes you end up receiving or using some text that has various codes in it that Word doesn't understand.

Many formatting codes use greater than (<) and less than (>) signs. These symbols are what you get when you type Shift+, (comma) or Shift+.(period).

For example, not too long ago I ended up needing to extract some text from an RTF file that crashed and couldn't be read as RTF anymore. Like HTML and XPress tags, RTF uses greater than and less than signs to signify formatting. If you read in an RTF file as plain text, you get lots of creepy formatting codes in addition to the text you are trying to extract. The same thing happens if you look at plain HTML (right-click and choose View|Source on any Web page and you'll see what I mean).

So today, I wanted to extract the text out of my corrupted RTF file. I needed to remove the formatting information, so I would be left with just plain text. I didn't want to laboriously remove the codes by hand, so I knew I needed to search and replace for text in between greater than and less than signs.

Because I didn't know exactly what text would be in between the codes, I knew I needed to use Word XP's "wildcard" feature. The online help explains how you use the asterisk (*) wildcard to search for a string of characters. For example, if you type in s*d, the search and replace finds both sad and started.

The bad news is that in Word, the greater than and less than signs also mean something special in the Find and Replace box (they mean the beginning or end of a word). So, after much experimentation, I finally found out that if I want the greater than and less than signs not to be read as special codes, I had to put a backslash in front of them. So to ditch the codes, what I finally ended up doing was the following:

1. Choose Edit|Replace.

2. Click the More button and check Use wildcards.

3. Put \<(*)\> into the Find What box and leave the Replace with box blank. But use the real greater than and less than characters.

4. Click Find Next, Replace, or Replace All.

Word goes through and takes out all the codes. Since I'm not a programmer, figuring this out was a small technological triumph!

Fun with Text

A reader asked: "I have a one-year old Dell computer with Windows XP. I am looking for a program that lets you do fancy printing and write in a wavy line."

When I read this, I immediately thought of WordArt. Given that the reader has a Dell, the computer probably came preloaded with either Microsoft Office or Microsoft Works. In either case, within the word processing program, there's a small extra program called WordArt. Usually it's a button on a toolbar that looks like a slanted capital A. With that tool, you can make text that's wavy or has other effects.

Here's how you use WordArt in Word. First, you need to show the Drawing toolbar if it's not already on your screen. Choose View|Toolbars and click to place a checkmark next to Drawing. A new toolbar appears at the bottom of your screen. Towards the middle of the toolbar, you'll see the slanted A WordArt button. (If you have ScreenTips turned on and hold your mouse over the button, it says Insert WordArt.)

To use Word Art, click the button and follow these steps:

1. In the Word Art gallery dialog box, click to select a style of text.

2. Click OK.

3. Type your text in the dialog box. You can change the font and size as well.

4. Click OK.

Your text appears over the document along with the WordArt toolbar. You can use the various buttons on the toolbar to change the appearance. For example, you can change the text and control how the document text wraps around the WordArt. If you decide not to use it after all, you can just click to select the WordArt and press the Delete key to remove it.

Creative Bullets in Word

Pretty much everyone who uses Microsoft Word knows how to create a bullet. You put your cursor in the line of text that you want bulleted and press the Bullets button on the Formatting toolbar. Voila, your line has a bullet in front of it.

But what if you don't like the plain old boring round dot? A lot of people don't realize that Word gives you a lot more options than just the dot. With your cursor in the bulleted line, choose Format, Bullets and Numbering. In the dialog box that appears the plain ole black dot is the one that is selected. You can click one of the bullet styles in the other boxes to select a different style.

If you want to get creative, click the Customize button. In Word XP, you'll see three buttons: Font, Character, and Picture. (In Word 2000 and earlier, you see these options in other areas of the Bullets and Numbering dialog box.)

If you click the Font button, you enter a standard Font dialog box. You change the font attributes for your bullet the same way you'd change text anywhere else in Word. In this dialog box, you can change the size of your bullet character and even make it bold or change the color of your bullet.

If you click the Character button, you can see all of the characters available to you in the Symbol font. You'll notice that this dialog box looks a lot like Windows' Character Map utility program. It works the same way; you can choose any character just by double clicking it. Or you can choose another font from the drop-down box to check out the characters in other symbol-type fonts such as Wingdings or Webdings.

If you click the Picture button, Word presents you with a whole slew of clip art bullets in all sizes, shapes, and colors.

After you have the bullet formatted the way you like, click OK and you'll see your new, more creative bullet in your text. If you plan to use your special bullet a lot, you even may want to include it as part of a style.

Creating Lines in Word

In my time, I have seen many ugly forms and documents created in Word. One of the most egregious document bloopers I see is uneven or broken horizontal lines. Bad lines in a document are a sure sign of someone attempting to use Word like a typewriter.

Using Word like a typewriter is at best time-consuming and at worst frustrating. For example, suppose you want to create a line at the top of your document. Many books or reports put a line below the book title or chapter that appears at the top of the page. If you try to do this using the underline character on your keyboard, it won't work well at all.

But there is a better way. Actually, you can create lines that have nothing to do with the underline character in several ways:

1. Put a border on your text.

2. Create a table with a line on only one side.

3. Use the line tool on the Drawing toolbar.

For example, to create your line in your header, choose View|Header and Footer. Now type your book title and highlight it. Choose Format|Borders and Shading. In the Borders tab, select your line options from the drop down lists and click where you want the border in the Preview area. In the Apply to drop-down, be sure to click Paragraph, and click OK.

If you wanted to create a line under three words with one word left justified, one centered, and one right justified, your best bet would be to use a table. Choose Table|Insert|Table and create a one row table with three columns. Type each word into a cell and left, center, or right justify it in the cell. Now choose Format|Borders and Shading and add a bottom border.

Finally, if you need to create a diagonal line or some other line that can't be done another way, you can use the Line tool on the Drawing toolbar. Just be aware that because it's a free-floating line, it can take quite a bit of time to adjust it correctly with your mouse, so the line ends up where you want it.

Backing Up Office Settings

Recently a reader wrote in to ask about the best way to save her Word settings because her company is planning to upgrade their computer systems. She knew that most settings in Word are saved in the Normal.dot template, and (correctly) figured that saving that file aside is a good idea. But she wasn't sure if her macros would be saved too.

Because I never throw anything away, I still have templates that I created in Word 6 long, long ago. Saving your templates aside is actually easy. The hardest part is finding out where Word stores your templates. So before you get your new computer, on your current computer, open Word and choose Tools|Options. Then click the File Locations tab. Next to Templates, you see the full path that tells you where your templates are stored on your hard disk. In new versions of Word, the path may be rather long deep within the Documents and Setting folder. You can just use Windows Explorer to navigate to that folder and save the template files or even the entire folder off to a floppy or CD. All your templates are now backed up, which is definitely a good thing. After you install Word on the new computer, you can just copy them to the Template folder there. (Again, you can just look in the File Locations tab to figure out where it the templates have been installed.) Macros are stored in templates, so if you save aside your templates, you get your macros too.

If you don't like the direct approach, and you have a recent version of Office, you also can use a built-in tool that comes with Office, which backs up the settings for all your Office applications. The Save My Settings Wizard saves the settings for the elements of Office you choose. Before you start, close any Office applications you might have running. Then click Start|Programs|Microsoft Office Tools and click the Save My Settings Wizard. Go through the wizard by clicking the Next button and tell it to Save the settings to a file. Click the Browse button to find a (preferably memorable) location on your hard disk to store your settings. Give the file a name and click Save.

Again, you can use Windows Explorer to copy this file off to a floppy or CD. Then you just take it to your new computer, copy the file onto the new hard disk and use the same wizard to restore the settings.

Word's Work Menu

The other day, I ran across a hidden Word gem that I've never seen before. It's an extra menu you can include to access documents you use often. Most people know about the "recently used documents" list at the bottom of the File menu. By default, this menu is set to show the last 4 documents you opened. You can change this number up to a maximum of 9 by choosing Tools|Options. In the General tab, make sure there's a checkmark next to Recently used file list and change the entry to a higher number.

Okay, that's sort of a side tip to my main tip, which is about the little-known Work menu. You can add this menu for those documents you access frequently, but that tend to fall off your recently used documents list. For example, I have a little Weekly Planning Form that I print out every Monday. There's no way it's still on my recently used documents list after a whole week. If I add the Work menu, I can put that file on it and still get to it quickly.

To add the menu, follow these steps:

1. Choose Tools|Customize.

2. In the Commands tab, under Categories, click Built-in menus.

3. Under Commands, scroll down and at the bottom you'll find Work.

4. Drag the Work menu to your menu bar.

Now you have a new menu with one item that somewhat cryptically says "Add to Work menu." To add a file, open the file you want first. Then Choose Work|Add to Work menu. Now you'll see your file listed in the menu. To access your file, you now can just choose the file name from the Work menu.

Getting a file off the Work menu is a little less intuitive, but it is possible. To delete a file, you need to press Ctrl+Alt+ - (that's the hyphen/minus sign). Your cursor turns into a big black minus sign. Now click the Work menu to open it and then click the file in the list you want to remove.

This last step is actually kind of dangerous because if you click incorrectly you can remove the wrong thing. Whatever you do, do NOT do what I did. While my cursor was a minus sign, I actually clicked on the Customize menu. It disappeared. The bad news is that if you have no Customize menu item, you can't restore the Customize menu item. It's a rather nasty Catch-22.

Because I did such an incredibly dumb thing, I had to take drastic action. Here's what you can do if you find yourself in such a predicament. Determine where your Normal.dot template is located by choosing Tools|Options. In the File Locations tab, you can see where your templates are on your hard disk. Then choose File|Exit to get out of Word.

Now using Windows Explorer, go to your templates folder and rename Normal.dot to Normal-old.dot. Open Word and it will reappear with its default version of the Normal template, which includes all the menus. If you need styles or macros from the old template you can use the Organizer to load them into your new Normal.dot.

Show Full Pathname

Recently, a reader wrote and told me about a number of her pet peeves with Microsoft Word. She's a long-time Word Perfect user who only uses Word under duress. The reality of the word processing world is that for file compatibility, it helps to use the same word processor everyone else does. Sad but true.

As I've mentioned before, I used Word Perfect long before I used Word. Moving to Word was a horrible transition. In any case, our long-suffering reader had a gripe that I'd never thought about before.

Word Perfect shows you the entire pathname in the title bar of the window. Word only shows you the document name, not the full path. If you have the same file stored in multiple folders, you can't tell them apart.

There are Word macros you can write or obtain that will put the full pathname in the title bar. However, here's an easy workaround for the problem that doesn't require a macro. The full pathname of your file appears if you display the Web toolbar by choosing View|Toolbars|Web. The toolbar has an Address button that looks much like the address bar in a Web browser. If you don't want a whole bunch of toolbars cluttering your screen, you also can just add the Address button from the Web toolbar onto your Standard toolbar so it's near the top. To add the button you can choose View|Toolbars|Customize and drag the button over.

Set File Locations in Word

If you've read my tips before, you may have noticed that I have an aversion to the MyDocuments folder. I think it's stupid, much like Microsoft Bob or endless Windows animation. Let's just say that I don't like to have my file organization dictated by some nerd at Microsoft. I mean really, obviously, if it's my computer, those are my documents. Duh. I don't need a folder to tell me that. So I never use it. That folder is empty. Forever.

However, making this personal statement against MyDocuments means I have to tell every piece of Microsoft software where I do want to put my files. Other software commits what I view as an even more heinous act. By default, certain software products will try to save their data files into the same folder as the software. As I've mentioned in the past, mingling your software and your data is a bad idea, assuming you ever want to find or back up your files easily.

Most "lost" files stem from people just clicking Save before they noticed where exactly they were saving the file. So, here's a tip: force the software to put files in a particular location. Most software has some kind of location for "preferences" like where you want to put your files.

For example, in Microsoft Word, choose Tools|Options and click the File Locations tab. Under File Types, note the location where Word wants to save your documents. This location may not be where YOU want to put your files, so you either misplace them or spend a lot of time navigating your hard disk trying to put the file where you want it. But you can change this default location easily. With the Documents line highlighted, click the Modify button. Now navigate to a folder where you keep your documents.

For example, for years I have kept my project data on a separate drive and separate folder from the rest of my computer. So on my system Word points to D:\proj. It's likely that I'll be saving documents into a subfolder off this folder, so saving files goes a lot more quickly than if I had to navigate from My Documents over to the D drive.

Modifying Word

A reader asked a good question the other day. She asked "I recently switched from Word Perfect to Word. In WP I had an icon on my regular toolbar that took me to graphics and it was fairly easy to add any feature, shortcut, or macro I desired to the toolbar. But there isn't any clip art (or graphics/picture) on the Word toolbar. I've read the Help menu and experimented with the instructions they give for adding a feature to the tool bar, but have had no success in doing so. Any suggestions?"

Many people think that their application software can't be changed. Not true. There are two answers to this question. In Word, the easiest thing you can do is show the Picture toolbar, which has the Insert Picture command on it. To do that, choose View|Toolbars and click to put a checkmark next to Picture. The little yellow button is Insert Picture. (If they aren't showing, you may want to turn on "ScreenTips" which are the little yellow text that pops up and says what each button does. (I love the little tips because I can never remember which button does what!) To show ScreenTips, choose View|Toolbars|Customize. Click the option Tab and put a checkmark next to Show ScreenTips on toolbars.

The larger answer is that you can put any Word command onto any toolbar or create your own new toolbars with all your favorite commands on them. Choose Tools|Customize command. Click the Commands tab and select a category. Next, drag the button to the toolbar you want to modify. If you change your mind, you can drag the buttons back off the toolbar to remove them. You can rearrange the buttons by dragging them into a new position. Be careful when dragging and dropping buttons -- if you drag one button on top of an existing button, Word thinks you are replacing the button, which may or may not be what you intended to do.

If you do a search in the online help on "Toolbar" you can find more information on creating your own toolbars too.

Add Buttons to the Word Toolbar

Every time I teach a class on Word, I remember why I changed the toolbar. The default installation of Word includes toolbar buttons that I never use. Years ago, I changed them and I've never looked back. Every time I upgrade Word, it finds my modified toolbar, so I've never had to think about it again.

For example, on my personalized Word toolbar, I have a button called "Word Count." This button comes in handy for articles like this one that need to be a certain length. Instead of choosing the command from the Tools menu, I just click a button. Here's how I added it to the toolbar. First, you choose Tools|Customize and click the Commands tab. You'll see a list of Categories. These categories correspond to the Word menus. Since we know that the Word Count command is in the Tools menu, you click the Tools category. Now scroll down until you find the Word Count command.

Now, click and drag the Word Count command to a toolbar. I put it at the end of the Standard toolbar (at the top, closest to the menus). But you can add the button to any toolbar that is visible on your screen. It will show the name of the command, but you can change it to something else if you prefer. If you want to change your button, click the Modify Selection button in the Customize dialog box.

Depending on how you use Word, you may find that you want buttons for commands that don't appear in the menus. If you don't see the command you are looking for in a particular category, click All Commands in the Categories box. You'll see every available Word command.

While you have the Customize dialog box open, you also can easily remove buttons. If adding all those buttons makes your toolbar too crowded, just click and drag the buttons you don't want off the toolbar. And voila, you have a useful toolbar that only includes the stuff you use and doesn't include the stuff you don't use.

Change Word Back

As I've mentioned before, I've used Word for a long time. And most things in Word are the same old stuff. However two things have changed so radically in recent versions that they totally drive me nuts: mail merge and styles. Now when you use these features you are presented with the Task Pane. As far as I'm concerned the jury is still out on the whole Task Pane concept. Maybe it's just because I'm not used to it, but mostly it seems like it just gets in the way.

Anyway, I whined about my problems to a Word guru friend of mine and she told me what I could have probably guessed: if you don't like it, just change it back.

I've pointed out many times that if you don't like something about Word, odds are you can change it. Well, I should have taken my own advice. If you like the old mail merge feature, here's how you get it back.

1. First show the Mail Merge Toolbar by choosing View|Toolbars and clicking Mail Merge.

2. Choose Tools|Customize and make sure you are in the Commands tab.

3. Under Categories, click All Commands.

4. Now under Commands click MailMergeHelper and drag it to the Mail Merge toolbar. If you also want it on the menu, drag it to the Tools menu (where it used to be).

5. When you are done, click the Close button in the Customize dialog box.

Adding the old style dialog box works the same way. Follow steps 2 and 3. Once you are in the Customize dialog box, click the FormatStyle command and drag it over to the Format menu where it used to be.

Close the Customize dialog box and you'll find that suddenly a few things look a whole lot more familiar.

Making Text Stay Together

You've probably experienced the thrill of printing a document and discovering that you have a line of text where it doesn't belong. The technical term for a single line or a couple of words that ends up at the top of the next page is a widow. An orphan is a first line of a paragraph that ends up as the last line of a page or column. Neither situation is good.

The problem is that Word's automatic page breaks sometimes fall where you don't want them. Widows and orphans aren't the only document problems you'll encounter either. For example, if your document has headings, you don't want a heading to end up on a different page than the text that goes with it. And if you have a bulleted list, you don't want one sad, lonely bullet left off by itself.

Fortunately, Word has widow and orphan controls enabled in the Normal style by default. So if you're one of those people who never peek into the world of styles and no one else messes with the Normal style, widows and orphans may never be a problem for you. You can check by choosing Format|Paragraph and clicking the Line and Page Breaks tab. Widow/Orphan control should have a checkmark next to it.

The Paragraph dialog box can help in those other situations too. For example, to keep your bullets together, just highlight the list and choose Format|Paragraph. In the Line and Page Breaks tab, click next to Keep lines together and all your bullets now travel as a unit.

If you have two paragraphs that always have to stay together, like a heading and it's related text, highlight the first paragraph and choose Format|Paragraph again. In the Line and Page Breaks tab, click the Keep With Next check box.

Of course, for maximum flexibility, you also can do the opposite and punt text off a given page. Instead of adding a lot of hard page breaks by pressing Ctrl+Enter, you can use the Page Break Before command. For example, suppose you have a figure that you want to be on a page by itself. To force Word to add a page break, place your cursor in the paragraph that contains the figure, choose Format|Paragraph and click the Line and Page Breaks tab. Then click the Page Break Before check box.

Add Comments to Documents

I've done a lot of editing for a lot of years, and one command we editors know about is Word's Comment feature. Pretty much every version has some iteration of Comments, but few people use them. However, in certain circumstances, it can be extremely useful. In situations where multiple people need to share documents and make revisions, being able to explain your changes or add queries can come in handy.

The beauty of comments is that they are actually hidden from the main body of the Word document. Early versions of Word called them Annotations and you had to view them using a menu command. In Word 2000 Comments displayed like a little on-line Post-It note, whenever you move your cursor over the highlighted text. In Word 2003, comments appear alongside the text.

To add a comment, highlight a range of text. Now choose Insert|Comment and you'll see the text you selected is highlighted in color (like with a highlighter pen) and a bubble appears with your initials. You type your peerless prose next to them. (Note that the initials information that appears in the pane can be changed by choosing Tools|Options and clicking the User Information tab.) You can show or hide comments by choosing View|Markup.

When you insert comments the Reviewing toolbar appears. Sometimes comments can get long and if you want to see all of the text, you can show the Reviewing pane by clicking the button. I've found over the years that if you have a lot of comments (i.e., revisions to revisions and multiple explanations), sometimes it's easier to just leave the Reviewing pane open while you are reading and work with the comments somewhat like on-screen footnotes.

Because the comments are hidden text, they don't print out unless you specifically tell Word to do so. To print your document with comments, choose File|Print and change the Print What drop-down box to Document Showing Markup.

Set Up Envelopes in Word

Every time I publish a magazine, I send out checks to writers afterward. The checks go out to more or less the same people every time, although the group has grown over the years. At some point, hand-writing the envelopes got to be a bit of a pain. Plus, we ran out of pre-printed envelopes and I'm too cheap to get more printed, especially when people just throw envelopes away.

If I'm writing a letter, I'll often use Word's Envelope and Labels command to do a quick envelope. All you have to do is highlight the return address in your letter and chose Tools | Envelopes and labels. The address appears in the Delivery Address box, ready to go. All you have to do is put an envelope in the printer and click Print.

But with multiple envelopes, this process becomes cumbersome. You could do a mail merge, but that seems sort of silly for 5 or 6 envelopes. The best thing is to just set up a document that contains all your envelopes with addresses. So in my case, I created a new document called Writer_Envelopes. doc.

The trick is setting the page size correctly. In the Word world, each envelope is a new page. Choose File|Page Set up to set it up correctly. Your margins will depend on whether you want to include your return address or not. If you have a stamp or preprinted envelopes and don't want to include a return address, in the Margins tab, set the top margin to 1.5 inches, the bottom margin to .5 inches, the left margin to 4 inches and the right margin to 1 inch.

In the Paper Size tab, change the drop-down to Com 10 Envelope and the orientation to Landscape. In the Paper Source tab, change the source to Manual or Envelope feeder, if your printer has one.

If you decide to import your logo or include a return address, set the top and left margins to .5 or even a little less, depending on how close your printer can print to the edge of the page. You also should create a style or format your address text with a left indent of 4 inches.

Type your addressee information into the envelope and press Ctrl+Enter to add a new page (i.e. envelope) to the document. When you're done, put some envelopes into the printer and start printing away. Because you can save the file, the next time you have to run the same bunch of envelopes, all you have to is open the file and print.

Creating Label Sets in Word

In the previous tip, I wrote about how you can create and save a Word file for envelopes you use repeatedly. Another fast way to save recurring address information is to use labels. Basically you just create a sheet of address labels with all your addresses in them, print them out, and peel them off.

This is a great technique if you pay a number of bills where the company you're paying doesn't provide a preprinted envelope. I've written before about how you can do labels using a mail merge, but never about how you create a plain old document filled with labels.

The main thing to realize is that a sheet of "labels" is really just a Word table that has had its margins, rows, and columns set so that the text lines up correctly on a sheet of peel-and-stick labels. The dialog box includes the standard Avery and other name-brand product numbers, but you don't have to buy any particular brand of labels. (Yes, you can buy the cheap office supply store brand and it won't make any difference!) You just need to know the measurements of the label you have.

To create a page of labels in Word 2003, you choose Tools|Letters and Mailings|Envelopes and Labels. (In Word 2000, the command is just Tools|Envelopes and Labels.) Now click the Label tab and click the Options button to set the label type. You can change the Label product drop-down to your label brand and find the number. Or you can find an equivalent in the list. Just click a product number on the left and you'll see what size the individual labels are. Many generic brands of labels also say somewhere on the box that they are "equivalent" to a particular Avery number.

When you're done setting options, click OK. Back in the Envelopes and Labels dialog box, make sure the Print radio button is set to Full page of the same label. Now click the New Document button and all the labels appear on the page. As I said, it's just a Word table, so you can type your own text and save the file like you would any other document.

Create a Table of Contents in Word

Many people think that creating a table of contents in Word is some mystical woo-woo amazing task that only a chosen few can figure out. But generating a basic table of contents is actually quite simple. The trick is that you need to format your text with styles.

A style lets you name a group of formatting attributes and apply them all at once. For example, if you want your headings to be bold Arial 12 point, rather than format each one individually, you create a style that has all those attributes in it. Then you apply the style to all your headings. Whether you realize it or not, every particle of text in a document is in fact formatted with a style: the Normal style.

Word comes with a number of built-in styles other than Normal. It has styles named Heading 1, Heading 2 and so forth up to Heading 7. Even if you normally don't use styles, you want to learn about the heading styles to create a table of contents.

To apply a built-in heading style, place your cursor in the text you want to change and choose the style name from the Style drop-down on the Formatting toolbar.

After you have applied the built-in heading styles to your text, you can generate a table of contents. The concept is simple. Word takes the text in the paragraph that has the heading style, figures out what page it is on to create a table of contents entry.

So to make Word generate the table of contents, place your cursor at the point you want Word to insert it. Then in Word 2000 choose Insert | Index and Tables (in Word XP select Reference | Index and Tables) and click the Tables of Contents tab. Click the Formats drop-down to change the appearance and click the Show Levels number to change the number of heading levels Word will use to generate the table of contents. Click OK and Word magically creates the table of contents.

Create a Shortcut to a Font

I have a lot of fonts on my system, so my font selection box in Word is very long. I end up doing quite a bit of scrolling to find the font I want. However, it doesn't have to be that way. In Word, you can set up a keyboard shortcut so you can apply a font with just a keystroke.

For example, I lay out many of our books using a font called Warnock Pro, and I often want letters and other collateral materials to be formatted using the same font, so they match. Scrolling down to Warnock Pro is kind of a drag since it starts with W. One quick trick you can use is to click the down arrow next to fonts on the Formatting toolbar, so it pops down. Then type the letter of the font name (W in this case). Word jumps your cursor down to the Ws.

Although this trick works okay, a keyboard shortcut is still much quicker because I have many versions of Warnock on my system (Warnock Pro Caption, Warnock Pro Display, etc.). Typing the letter only takes you to the first font name that starts with the letter. Plus, if you've selected a "w" font recently, Word places it at the top, so you have to resort to scrolling down to find the rest of your Ws if you want a different version.

Here's how you set up the keyboard shortcut:

1. Choose Tools|Customize and click the Commands tab.

2. Click the Keyboard button

3. Look under Categories and then click Fonts.

4. In the Fonts area, find the font you want (Warnock Pro in my case).

5. Next to Press New Shortcut key, type a key combination you want to use for the shortcut (I used Alt+W). If the keyboard shortcut has already been assigned to something, Word will warn you. (It's not a good idea to overwrite any default shortcut that you might want to use later.)

6. Click Assign and then Close the dialog boxes.

Now, when I want to change the font to Warnock Pro, I just highlight the text and press Alt+W. It's easy!

Hidden Menu Shortcut

I tend to use the same programs on an almost daily basis. Many times I wish that one software product had a small feature that is available in another. For example, both Corel Draw and Microsoft Word have a "repeat the last thing I just did" shortcut key. (The shortcut is Ctrl+R in Corel and Ctrl+Y in Word.) I basically wish EVERY program had that feature. Realistically, if you do something once, you might want to do it again.

Along the same lines, Macromedia (now Adobe) Dreamweaver has two menu items I use all the time. Save All and Close All. Because I have a lot of HTML files open at once, they are extremely handy commands, especially at the end of the day when I want to save, bail out of everything. and step away from the computer.

Word is another program I almost always have open. It's always sort of annoyed me that there's no Save All or Close All options, since I often have quite a number of Word files open at a given time. As an aside, here's another keyboard shortcut, use Ctrl+F6 to switch among your open documents.

Yes, I could customize the menus, but I never bothered. But as it turns out Word has a hidden way to access the Save All and Close All menu options. If you hold down the Shift key while you click the File menu, there they are! If you use other Office programs, try this trick in those applications too.

Replacing Special Characters

Every once in a while, someone asks me if you should place one space or two after a period at the end of a sentence. The answer is one. Putting two spaces after a period is an archaic holdover from typewriter days before we had proportional fonts.

However, every once in a while, I also have to deal with a document written by someone who doesn't know this small rule of typography. The document is filled with a whole lot of extra spaces that need to be removed. Fortunately, in Microsoft Word it's easy to find and replace non-printing characters like spaces.

In fact, you can tell Word to search and replace even more obscure items like section breaks and paragraph returns as well.

To find and replace spaces, you don't need to do anything fancy. Choose Edit|Replace and type two spaces into the Find What box. Yes, you place your cursor in the box and press your space bar two times. You won't see anything, since it's a space, but that's okay. In the Replace box, type one space. Click Find Next and Word finds the first occurrence of two spaces. Click Replace. If you want to do them all at once, click Replace All.

To find other non-printing characters, you again use the Replace dialog box. Click the More button and the Replace dialog enlarges with a lot more options. Click the Special button and you see a whole laundry list of items you can find. Click to select an item and Word puts a special code into the Find field. Of course, once you've done this a few times, you figure out what the codes are. For example, I often need to search for two paragraph returns and replace them with one. The special code for paragraph is ^p, so I just put it into the Find what box myself.

Creative use of the Replace dialog box can save a tremendous amount of time. The next time you find yourself laboriously changing something in a document, see if there's a way you can use the Replace function instead.

Paste Unformatted Macro

I write a weekly newsletter for a client that involves surfing technology news sites and then writing little "blurbs" about the latest happenings. In the process, I end up pasting a lot of quotations from articles on Web pages. The problem with pasting from the Web into Word is that you get all the formatting along with it. As I've written in the past, if you want to remove formatting, you have two options:

1. Highlight the offending text and press Ctrl+spacebar. This command removes all local formatting, so all you are left with is the formatting that is set up in the style.

2. Instead of doing a regular Paste, by pressing Ctrl+V, choose Paste Special. In the dialog box that opens, click Unformatted Text. Then only the text is pasted without any formatting.

I often use option 2, since I hate slowing down to fuss with formatting when I'm writing. It's easier for me to edit if I'm not distracted by some hideous purple font or something. Getting at the Paste Special dialog box is slow, so I put a button on my toolbar for it.

Even a button is still slower than using Ctrl+V, however and that bugs me. There is no simple way to access the Paste Special/Unformatted command directly because you have to choose it as an option in the dialog box. In this case, nothing short of a macro would do (but don't worry; it's easy). To create it, follow these steps. (NOTE: if you're using Word 2003, also see the note at the end of the article.)

1. Highlight some text in a document and press Ctrl+C to copy it. (You need to have text on the clipboard for the macro to work.)

2. Choose Tools|Macro|Record New Macro.

3. In the Macro Name box, enter a name for your macro like PasteUnformattedText. Click OK.

4. You see the tiny macro recording toolbar on your screen. It's recording now, so you don't want to make any extra moves.

5. Choose Edit|Paste Special and click the Unformatted Text radio button. Click OK to close the dialog box.

6. Now click the square Stop button on the Macro toolbar to make it stop recording.

With that, you have a macro! To try it out, choose Tools|Macro|Macros, select PasteUnformatedText from the list and click Run. Whatever you had on the clipboard is pasted in at your cursor location.

Now that you've proved it worked, adding a keyboard shortcut makes it just as fast as our old friend Ctrl+V. Choose Tools|Customize and click the Keyboard button. Under Categories, scroll down until you find Macros. Scroll down to find your PasteUnformattedText macro name on the right hand side. In the in the Press new shortcut key box, type a new key combination. I used Alt+V, because it's similar to Ctrl+V.

Editor's Note: Although this technique works in many versions of Word, due to a problem with the Word 2003 macro recorder, following the steps above may not record a macro that really pastes unformatted in Word 2003.

If it doesn't work, you need to go into the macro itself by choosing Tools|Macros|Macros. Select the macro from the list and click Edit. You will see the code. In between the Sub and End Sub lines, replace the code that is there with this code:

```
Selection.PasteSpecial Link:=False, DataType:=wdPasteText, Placement:= _
    wdInLine, DisplayAsIcon:=False
```

Then save and return to Microsoft Word.

New Highlighting Trick

Even though much of Microsoft Word looks and acts the same as it has for at least a decade, sometimes I run across new or changed features.

For example, here's a neat new trick, which I'm sure I never would have discovered myself, so it's a good thing I read about it first. In older versions of Word you couldn't highlight text that wasn't contiguous. In other words, you could only click and drag to highlight text all in a line or block.

However, now in recent versions of Word, you can highlight areas of text that are not next to each other. For example, suppose you are writing a press release about your great new plant, the Ultra Daffodil. Every time the word Ultra Daffodil appears, you want it to be bold so it stands out from the rest of the text.

The trick is the Ctrl key. In the imaginary press release, for example, you'd highlight the first instance of Ultra Daffodil. Then while you hold down the Ctrl key on your keyboard, you'd highlight the next one, and so on until you have all the text you want highlighted. (Be sure you don't let up on that Ctrl key until you're done.)

Once you have the text highlighted, then you can click the Bold button on the toolbar or press Ctrl+B to bold all the instances of Ultra Daffodil that you highlighted. After you have highlighted the text, you can apply any number of changes to it; you aren't just limited to bold. For example, you could choose Format|Font and change all the instances of Ultra Daffodil to a completely different font that looks festive and evokes the feeling of Spring.

The end result is that you can make a lot of formatting changes with far fewer keystrokes, which I regard as a mighty fine thing.

Make Shortcuts to Templates

One of the secrets to a happy marriage is to have separate computers. In our computer-intensive household, this approach has worked well for many years. However, occasionally I do have to venture over into the other office to use my husband's computer because it's the only one that has QuickBooks loaded on it. Recently, I got to experience James' workspace for a bit, and I noticed his desktop had some extra shortcuts.

I suppose that sometimes it's good to get out of your own little world and see how other people use their computers. On my computer, most of my shortcuts go to software programs. But as I've written before, a shortcut can point to pretty much anything on your computer, including files or folders. James has shortcuts that point to Microsoft Word templates that he uses frequently.

Pointing a shortcut to a template is easy and can save you a lot of time. For example, many companies have specific Word templates set up for reports and other frequently used documents. Instead of opening a blank document in Word using that template, you can just create a shortcut on your desktop. Then when you double-click the shortcut, Word dutifully opens a new document based on the template, so you can avoid wandering around the New dialog box or Task Pane.

To create a shortcut to a Word template, you need to find out where Word has stored them. This location may depend on your version of Word and whether or not you are using a network. To find out, from within Word choose Tools|Options.

Click the File Locations tab and note the folder that's next to User Templates.

Now to create your shortcut:

1. Right-click in an empty spot on your desktop.

2. Choose New|Shortcut from the pop-up menu.

3. Click the Browse button and navigate to the folder where you discovered Word is storing your templates.

4. In that folder, click the filename for the template you want and click Next.

5. Enter a descriptive name for your shortcut, so you'll remember what it's for, and then click Finish.

Now with your spanky new shortcut, you are just one double-click away from a new document!

Finding and Highlighting

As I've noted in the past, some aspects of more recent versions of Word give me a big pain. So for small tasks like writing articles, I tend to just revert back to Word 2000, which is faster and less filled with annoyances like the Task Pane, which I detest.

However, newer versions of Word do have a feature that is completely cool. Over the years, I've spent a lot of quality time using Find and Replace to quickly fix many problem documents. But when you do a big replace, there's also a big risk. You can make a mess if you're not careful. Sometimes you confidently click the Replace button and serious badness ensues when you discover later that you replaced a bunch of stuff that you really shouldn't have.

Anyway, new versions of Word have a new check box in the Find dialog box that says "Highlight all items." So before you do something drastic you can scroll through and see exactly what would be affected. For example, say you want to change every instance of the word "table" to "chair." If you highlight all items first, you'd see that the word "comfortable" now would become comforchair. Ooops. So you can go back and tweak your search to make it smarter (such as by clicking Find whole words only in the search options).

The highlight feature works because later versions of Word can highlight non-continuous text. So you can use Find and Replace to do other tricky things, such as pulling out pieces of your document. For example, many times I have wanted to pull out just the headings from a document. I thought you could do it in outline view, but in older versions, I couldn't. I'd try and copy just the headings, yet get everything.

Now you can do a search for anything tagged with a particular style, such as Heading 1. All the text is highlighted, so you can press Ctrl+C and copy it out to a new document. If you use character styles you can format particular terms using the style, then search for the character style and copy out the text. This technique would be a great way to gather the terms for a glossary or URLs for a Web index without having to resort to using bookmarks.

Editing in Print Preview

The other day one of my clients was working in Word and called me about a tip I told him about that he couldn't remember anymore. He has a document that has many lines in it and for some reason, they don't show up correctly in the standard Print Layout or Normal views. If the lines don't line up, he had to switch between Print Preview and Print layout to tweak them, deleting or adding underline characters.

Except he really doesn't have to because you can do simple editing in Print Preview.

This little known feature is great if you've ever spotted a last minute goof right before sending a file to the printer. You don't have to switch back to Normal view. Instead, in the Print Preview, take note of the little magnifier icon (to the right of the Print button). You might think it's just for zooming in, but it's also what makes it possible to edit. When you click the button, your cursor turns into an "I" beam so you can make changes.

Here's another tiny tip most Word users don't know. When working in tables, most people know that you can change row and column sizes, just by click and dragging the borders. But if you want them to be a particular size, it can be challenging to get them just right. However, if you hold down the Alt key while you drag or hold down both the left and right mouse buttons while you drag, Word shows you the dimensions in the ruler.

Even if you only save a few minutes with each of these tips, those minutes do add up over time. When it comes to Word, sometimes these little things can mean a lot.

Don't Check It

The other day, I amazed and astounded my husband, the nerd, with this cool tip. It's not easy to impress the nerd, so I figured I should share this one.

As most people know, I work on a lot of long technical tomes that are produced in Microsoft Word. Here's a little known fact: you can tell Word not to spell check certain parts of your document. At first you might wonder why that's a good idea, but this feature is actually extremely useful if you have something like programming code examples in your large technical document. Laboriously, spell checking pages of code and clicking the Ignore button 7,000 times is no fun.

Although it's not exactly intuitive, turning off spell checking for a particular passage of text is actually found in the Language settings. You can tell Word that text is in a foreign language and then it can use an alternate dictionary to spell check it. Or not check it at all.

So in this case, you could highlight your piece of programming code and choose Tools|Language|Set Language. In the Language dialog box, you don't change the language (i.e. you leave it set to English), but you click to add a checkmark next to "Do not check spelling or grammar."

Now here's the part that the resident nerd thought was really cool. If you use styles, you can set this no proofing language attribute within the style. Because all programming code in a book should look the same, the smart Word user creates a style to format it. Then in the Style dialog box for your Code style, click Modify, then Format, and then Language. You see the same Language dialog box and you can tell Word "Do not check spelling or grammar" for all your programming code with one quick click.

Automatically Update Text

Here's a cool Word tip that can come in handy if you have a lot of similar documents that use the same chunk of text which changes periodically. For example, suppose you have to create a series of contracts that all use a block of legalese. When the lawyers change their mind about what that verbiage needs to say, instead of having to go in and change every single contract, you can update all your contracts automatically just by updating the little block of text.

The key is to link the text block into the document. Instead of doing a regular "copy and paste" to put your text into the document, you create a separate file with the changeable block of text and do a "Paste Special" and link it in. To give it a try, follow these steps.

1. Create a document that has only the text that may change. In this example, it's the legalese paragraph. Save the file on your hard disk somewhere that you won't forget with a memorable name (like Legalese.doc).

2. Create the document that has all the other text, except for the text that may change. In this example, it would be the contract. Save the file with a name like CustomerContract.doc.

3. Open up Legalese.doc and choose Edit|Select All to select the entire contents. Now choose Edit|Copy.

3. In CustomerContract.doc, place your cursor at the point where you want to include the legalese paragraph.

4. Choose Edit|Paste Special. In the Paste Special Dialog box, select Paste Link.

The information in Legalese.doc can be copied as a link into as many contract files as you want. Then whenever the lawyers change their legal minds about what the legalese needs to say, you just open up one file (Legalese.doc), change the text, and all your contracts are updated. The only thing that you need to be careful about is moving the Legalese.doc file. If you move it, Word loses track of the link and you'll have to redo it. That's why it's good to save the file with the changeable text in a memorable and consistent location on your computer.

Excel Tips

I'm not much of an Excel guru, but there are times when even numerically challenged people like me need to use a spreadsheet to get work done. When you need to calculate, a spreadsheet is the way to go.

The truth is I stink at math. I'm not just talking calculus or higher math. No, I mean every type of math. Put a math problem in front of me and I'll find a way to mess it up. I am NOT the person you want anywhere near anything having to do with numbers.

In fact, one of my most vivid memories of kindergarten is looking at a number three and deciding that I really was afraid of threes. Twos were okay, but threes made me nervous. Having decided that, I gravitated back to the phonics exercises. (Yeah, for some of us, math phobia started really early.)

I still have a personal trauma every time I have to determine which stupid little sideways V is the greater than sign and which one is the less than sign. I've actually had math class nightmares about that kind of thing. It's like that old cliché dream where you are called up to the front of the class to solve some labyrinthine problem on the black board. Some people dream they are naked. For me being hopelessly mathematically impaired is embarrassing enough.

If you're like me and only use a spreadsheet when you really have to, these tips are for you. You won't find a bunch of formulas, just a few basic hints like what the cryptic #### means, and what to do when you can't get your printout to look decent.

Excel Cells

As noted, spreadsheets aren't a lot of fun if you aren't a numbers whiz. When you open a word processor, it's fairly obvious that you need to start typing words to make anything happen. It's less obvious what to do with all those boxes in a spreadsheet. In spreadsheet parlance, the little boxes are called cells. A cell is the intersection of a column and a row. Columns are named with letters, and rows are named with numbers, so a cell gets it's name from its column and row location, such as A1, which is the intersection of column A and row 1.

So, you type in numbers in your cells and then use Excel's formulas to perform mathematical operations on them. You use the cell names in your formulas. For example, suppose you wanted to add the contents of the first and second rows in your spreadsheet. So you type numbers in cells A1 and A2. Then you'd put your cursor in cell A3 (the third row in the first column). In the formula bar at the top of the window, you'd type =SUM(A1:A2) in the Excel formula bar.

Another handy feature is the ability to freeze rows and columns. As you create larger spreadsheets, you often aren't able to view all the column or row titles and the data at the same time. So to solve the problem, you can "freeze" rows or columns. For example, to Click the row number below where you want the split to be (or the column to the right of where you want the split) and choose Window|Freeze Panes. To remove the split, choose Window|Unfreeze Panes.

A Few Excel Tips

A while ago, I was doing some simple planning and "what if" type calculations in a spreadsheet. Although I don't use

Microsoft Excel particularly often, there are times when nothing but a spreadsheet will do. Because I don't use Excel much, I spend a lot of time reading the online help to remember how to use it. While trolling the help files, I found a couple of timesaving tips.

For example, in my spreadsheet, I had to enter the same number into several cells. I could have copied and pasted the number, but I found out there's an easier way. First you select the cells that should have this number. Now, while the cells are still selected, type your number into one of them. Press Ctrl+Enter and the number magically appears in all the cells you have selected. Note that the cells don't have to be a contiguous range either. You can select cells that aren't next to each other. To do that, instead of clicking and dragging to select a range, hold down the Ctrl key and click the cells you want to select.

In my baby spreadsheet, I also needed to enter a list of business names. Later on, I decided I wanted to put numbers in the column next to my list of names. Rather than typing in the information in each cell, I used Excel's ability to automatically fill in a series of numbers.

To do this, you type the number you want in the first cell of the range you want to fill (in this case, I typed a 1). Then enter a value in the next cell so Excel can figure out the pattern (in this case, 2). Now, select all the cells in the range you want to fill along with your two cells that have numbers. Now choose Edit|Fill|Series. In the dialog box, you can indicate how you want Excel to fill in your block. This technique also works with dates, so if you had a list of months you could start with January 2006 and Excel could figure out the rest of the year for you.

Excel Keyboard Tips

Sometimes things happen in Excel that seem mighty mysterious to me. Recently, I ran across a few tips that explained a few Excel oddities that I'd faced.

For example, here's one little tip I discovered all by myself. Sometimes I'm trying to enter something into an Excel cell and before I've committed myself to it, I realize that I've done something really dumb. Technically, I can't undo it because I haven't pressed the Enter key yet. But I want to restore the entry that was in the cell before I started doing something dumb. The answer is to press the Esc key. The previous cell contents are restored (what a relief).

Normally, when you type an equal sign (=) in Excel, it assumes you are going to follow that with a formula. Most of the time, that's a good thing. But here's an interesting problem: what if you really want to type an equal sign? Uh oh. The answer is that before you type your equal sign, you need to type an apostrophe, so that you enter '=. When you do this, you are telling Excel that you really are entering an equal sign and not a formula. Don't worry though, after you press Enter, the apostrophe disappears, so it doesn't display.

Here's one final Excel tidbit that's really pretty cool. Suppose you have a list of people who received invitations to a party. You want to add into a spreadsheet that they've either Accepted or Declined the invitation. Rather than typing the words Accepted or Declined endlessly, you can have Excel show you a drop-down list of the content that has previously been typed in a column.

Click the cell and then press Alt+Down Arrow. You see a list of all the entries that have been added in that column. Let go of the Alt key and use the up and down arrow keys to select the entry you want. Now press Enter.

Of course, if you only have two possible entries like the invitation example, this tip is only mildly exciting. But if you have a large spreadsheet with a lot of different, but repeating entries in a column, imagine how much time it could save!

Conditional Formatting in Excel

For math-phobes like me, formatting spreadsheets isn't generally as exciting as formatting text, but it is nonetheless extremely satisfying to have a spreadsheet look the way you want. As most people know, you can change font colors, and add borders and shading to Excel cells, much like you can in Word. In Excel, you choose Format|Cells and then select the various options in the tabs.

Recently, however I ran across a cool Excel formatting tip that isn't much like Word at all. Suppose you have a spreadsheet that shows fluctuating data such as stock prices or temperatures. You happily enter the data day after day, but over time you realize that it would be nice to easily spot the entries with data that is outside of a certain range.

For example, suppose you want to know every time the temperature went above 90 degrees this summer. In your spreadsheet, you have the high and low temperatures listed for each day. To make those 90+ degree days stand out, select the high temperature column and choose Format|Conditional Formatting.

In the dialog box that appears you can set what conditions the formatting will occur. So in this case, Set the Condition 1 drop-down to "Cell Value" then change the drop-down to the right of that to "greater than or equal to." Now in the third box, type in 90.

Next you click the Format button to tell it what you want it to display when the cell value is greater than 90. You can change the settings in the Font, Border or Patterns. For example, you could bold the font and change it to red and change the cell background to yellow to indicate it was hot on those days. When you're done, click OK and then OK again to exit the Conditional Formatting dialog box.

If you are really ambitious you can even set more than one condition. If you go back into the dialog box by choosing Format|Conditional Formatting again, you'll see the Add button. If you click it, you can go through the same process again.

Pasting Cells in Excel

When you copy cells in an Excel worksheet, the process is generally straightforward. You click and drag to select the cells you want to copy and press Ctrl+C or choose Edit|Copy.

Most of the time you just want to paste cells, so you press Ctrl+V to paste them in. But with a little exploration of the Paste Special dialog box, you may find that you have some other options that can make your life a lot easier.

For example, suppose you wanted to paste the columns from a spreadsheet as rows. Impossible you say? No, actually it's easy. The trick is to use Paste Special. Copy your column or columns and then click the first cell of the row where you want to place the data and choose Edit|Paste Special. Or you can right-click the cell and choose Paste Special. Either way, the Paste Special dialog box appears. Click Transpose and then OK. Now your column is a row. If you copied data from more than one column, the data from the column farthest to the left would be the first row, and subsequent rows would follow. So for example, column A could become Row 1, column B would become Row 2 and so forth.

Another cool way to use Paste Special is to copy the value of a cell without the underlying formula. Sometimes copying the formula to a new place can make a big mess, so when you copy it use Paste Special and click the Values radio button instead.

Here's another one. Many times when you copy carefully formatted data from one worksheet to another, you lose the column widths and everything ends up all squished up. Rather than painstakingly reformatting all those columns, paste with Paste Special instead. Choose the Column Widths radio button and you'll see that the columns come out fine.

You also can have Excel automatically calculate items as you paste. This one is a little tricky but can be useful. For example, if you copy a cell and then paste it onto another cell that has content in it, you can have Excel automatically add the two amounts together. For example, suppose cell A1 has the number 2 in it and cell B1 has the number 3 in it. Highlight A1 and press copy. Now click B1 right-click and choose Paste Special. In the Paste Special dialog box, under Operation click to select Add and click OK. Cell B1 now has a 5 in it. Pretty tricky, huh?

Make Excel Print the Way You Want

After you've got all those numbers entered and your formulas just right, you probably will want to print out your mathematical masterpiece. However, unlike Word, with Excel, what you see is very rarely what you get. I know that I've created many printouts with half a spreadsheet on one page and another half on another page. It's really annoying.

The trick to getting Excel to print what you expect is to use the Print Preview feature. Before you print out your worksheet, choose File|Print Preview to see what it will really look like when you print it. The preview shows headers and footers, and includes a status bar at the bottom of the window with the current page number and the total number of pages. (The total number of pages is often where I find a surprise -- what I thought was a small spreadsheet turns into four printed pages!)

In Print Preview, you see a number of buttons. Often changing the page orientation from portrait to landscape can make a spreadsheet print more nicely. Just click the Setup button and you'll find radio buttons you can click to change the page orientation. While you are looking at the preview you also can adjust the column widths. Click the Margins button and click and drag the handles to adjust the columns or the margins around the page to help make everything fit.

Another nifty thing in the Print Preview is the Page Break Preview. If you click this button, you can change where a page break occurs. Many times in a long spreadsheet, automatic page breaks occur in odd places. However, you can adjust the page breaks on the worksheet, so groups of related numbers stay together.

How Long Until Vacation

Here's a nifty use for Excel: figuring out how long it is until your next vacation. Excel can easily perform arithmetic on dates because it stores them as a plain old number. The next time you are moping in your cubicle wondering when you can head off to the Bahamas, you can fire up Excel, look like you're working and calculate how long it is until you are free. Here's how you do it. Suppose trip to the Bahamas begins on April 12, 2007 and today is November 16, 2006.

Excel stores dates as a regular serial number. In Excel's world view, time began on January 1, 1900. That was day one; January 2, 1900 was day 2, and so forth. To begin your calculations, type a date into cell A1. Excel understands slashes, so type 11/16/2006.

If you click in the cell and choose Format|Cells, you'll see Excel knows it is a date (the calculations won't work if the number is not formatted as a date). Now in cell A2, type in 4/12/2007. To find out how many days it is, you just do simple subtraction. In cell A3, type =A2-A1 to subtract November 16 from April 12. The result, however, is formatted as a date, which throws you off. Now, with your cursor in Cell A3, choose Format|Cells and change the type to General. You can now tell that the result is 147 days.

If you want to really get fancy, you can use one of Excels date formulas. For example, the NETWORKDAYS formula calculates how many work days there are between two days. In cell A4, type =NETWORKDAYS(A1,A2). You find that you have only 106 days of cubicle time left.

If you get an #NAME? error, it means you don't have the Analysis ToolPak add in installed. Choose Tools|Add Ins and see if it is in the list. If so place a check mark next to it. If you don't see any add-ins listed, you may need to install them from your Office CD.

Add the Calculator to Excel

I am not a numbers whiz, so when I use Excel, I always have a calculator standing by just in case. My formulas have an unhappy habit of coming up with "unexpected" results. Recently, I discovered that you can add a button that lets you access a calculator right from the Excel toolbar. This happy news means my ancient solar calculator can rest in a drawer while I'm fussing with formulas.

To add the calculator button:

1. Choose View|Toolbars and click Customize.

2. Click the Commands tab.

3. In the Categories list, click Tools

4. On the right hand side, under Commands, click Custom. (There are actually two icons that say Custom; you want the one that looks like a tiny gray calculator.)

5. Drag the little gray calculator button from the Commands list to a toolbar.

6. Click the Close button.

Now when you click the button, the Windows calculator runs. How convenient!

The curious among you may wonder what the other Custom button does. If you clicked the Description button in the Customize dialog box, you know that yes, the answer is

Solitaire. So if you really, really dislike Excel, you can add that button too and just go ahead and play Solitaire instead. (I did!)

What Does ##### Mean in Excel?

Using Excel is a challenge for me on a good day, and sometimes it does things that just mystify me. For example, after a long absence from Excel, I entered some information into a spreadsheet and ended up with #### in one of the cells instead of numbers.

I'd put in a formula and figured that I'd just done it wrong. (That would not be unusual for me after all.) Oddly enough, I couldn't find # (pound signs) in the online help. Maybe it's there, but I couldn't find it. Anyway, at some point, I finally discovered that it means the data is just too wide to fit in the cell. The annoying pound signs actually just indicate a formatting problem. You also may end up with your number turned into scientific notation, so a huge number turns into something like 1E+20.

Once you actually know what the pound signs mean, the solution is easy. You just need to make the column wider. The easiest way to make an entire column wider is to place your cursor at the top of the column and click and drag to move the column divider over. (You can tell when your cursor is in the right place and you are able to drag the divider when the cursor turns into a double-sided arrow.)

I'm also a big fan of Excel's AutoFit command, which automatically resizes the cells to fit the longest item in the column. Click on the letter at the top of the column to highlight the entire column. Then choose Format|Column|AutoFit Selection. An even easier way to access AutoFit is to double-click at the top of the column on the divider (again when the cursor is a double-sided arrow).

Once you make the column wider, magically all the pound signs go away.

PowerPoint Tips

Often people are introduced to presentation software under less than ideal circumstances. For one reason or another, you have to give a presentation. Now, in addition to the stress of having to give the presentation itself, you are faced with the task of learning a new piece of software as well. Not a pretty picture.

Your career could be riding on the professionalism of your presentation, but what if you aren't a graphic artist and you can't afford to hire one?

Fortunately PowerPoint is designed to be used by non-artists just like you and me. In fact, armed with a few tips, you might discover that creating your presentation is (dare I say it) *fun.*

If you are in the midst of a presentation crisis, you need to learn all you can learn about PowerPoint as quickly as possible. The tips in this section can help you get the job done quickly and easily.

Slide Graphic Tips

We've all seen bad PowerPoint presentations with cheesy graphics. They are just not pretty. Considering how important images are to your presentation, you should attempt to use the best graphics you can. Make sure that the images you use are appropriate for your audience.

Using cutesy or cartoony clip art may be okay for a very informal presentation, but in most cases you'll want to create or acquire good quality images that enhance your message rather than detract from it. (You don't want your audience marveling at how idiotic your clip art looks.) Also remember that, like words, images are protected by copyright law, so be sure that the images you use are royalty-free or you have paid for the right to use them.

You can insert two basic types of graphics: vector line art and bitmaps. Line art appears the same no matter what size you scale it because the lines are created using mathematical descriptions rather than by a pattern of dots (pixels) as they are in a bitmap. The number of dots in a bitmap (the resolution) determines how it will look at different sizes. If you scale up a low-resolution bitmap, it's possible to create a really ugly jagged effect.

If you use bitmap graphics, you need to consider whether or not you are creating slides or an onscreen presentation. If you are creating traditional slides, talk to your slide service bureau to find out what resolution they prefer.

For on-screen presentations, you want to size your graphics to work with the monitor you are using. Most laptop screens run at 1024x768, so a full-screen graphic should generally be 1024x768 at 96 dpi to look good on the screen. If you are creating smaller graphics, just do a little division. For example, a half page graphic would be 512 x 364 (1024 divided by 2 is 512 and 768 divided by 2 is 364).

Of course, the bottom line with any presentation is what it looks like. Practice your presentation beforehand to avoid any unwelcome surprises on "the big day."

PowerPoint Bullets

PowerPoint bullets are something everybody sees, but few do anything about. Bullets and numbers add interest to your presentation text, but you can make your lists more engaging if you venture beyond PowerPoint's standard default bullets and numbers. Windows comes with a number of fonts filled with bullet characters you can use. For even more options, you can use a clip art picture as a bullet character.

Using the default settings, you often end up with a gigantic bullet rammed right up next to the text, which looks somewhat absurd. However, it's easy to fix these unsightly problems by adjusting the spacing between the bullet and its text and changing the size of the bullet relative to its text.

First select your bullet text. Place your cursor anywhere in the paragraph you want to format. To format multiple paragraphs simultaneously, click and drag to highlight the text. The changes you make to bullets and numbers affect entire paragraphs even if you don't select all the text.

Now change the bullet character. Choose Format, Bullets and Numbering. Click the Bulleted tab and click Character. The Bullet dialog box appears. Choose a character set from the Bullets from drop-down box. Click a character and choose OK.

The amount of space between the bullet and the text is controlled by the indents setting. Make sure the Ruler is displayed (choose View|Ruler). Drag the left indent marker (the right-side up triangle) to the right to increase the hanging indent.

When you add a bullet to a slide, you may be surprised at how very large it is. In the Bulleted tab of the Bullets and Numbering dialog box, use the spin arrows to change the Size setting.

This option sets the bullet size as a percentage of the text size. A setting of 50-60% often looks much better than the default 100%.

Add Text Quickly Using Outline View

Over the years, I've watched a lot of people use PowerPoint. And I think I can safely say that a lot of presentations would take a lot less time if people entered their text using Outline View, rather than typing it directly into the slide. PowerPoint 97 had separate Outline and Slide views, so switching back and forth was kind of a pain. But now with PowerPoint 2000 (and later) in the standard Normal view, you can see the outline right next to your slides in a separate window "pane."

Adding text is a big part of creating any presentation. Generally to edit text in Slide view (or the Slide pane of Normal view), you click the sample text in a placeholder. The arrow cursor changes to an I-beam, which indicates you can start typing. This approach works okay if you are one of those people who prefers to type and format your text at the same time.

However, most people type first and format later, since it's hard to compose text if you are busy thinking about whether a word should be bold or not. So it's often easier to just blast out your presentation text first and not worry about the formatting until later

This situation is when entering text in Outline View (or the Outline pane of Normal view) can save you a lot of time. In the outline, you press the Enter key to add a new Slide title. Then you press Tab to demote an item, such as turning a slide title into a bullet point. You press Shift+Tab to promote an item, such as a turning a bullet point to a slide title. Pressing the

Enter key lets you continue typing text at the current level. For example, if you are typing a bullet and press Enter, you can type another bullet. It sounds confusing, but it's one of those things that makes sense when you try it out. Using just three keyboard commands, you can add text really quickly with absolutely no mousing around.

After you've input your text, it's easy to reorganize it in your outline later. Click the slide icon to the left of a slide heading and all the slide text is highlighted. Then you just click and drag the slide icon and text up or down the outline to a new location in your presentation.

Presentation Tricks

Most of us have sat through or given PowerPoint presentations. Often, it seems like something goes haywire. In a perfect world, you just press F5 to start the presentation. All your carefully crafted slides look lovely in full-screen Slide Show View as you seamlessly move through your topics. Unfortunately, in the real world, things rarely go perfectly.

The problem is that usually someone in the audience has a question about a topic that you either talked about earlier, or haven't gotten to yet. So you have to zap out of Slide Show View into PowerPoint, go into Slide Sorter View, and rummage around looking for the slide with the information you need. Retaining any sort of suave demeanor while you're rummaging like this is just about impossible.

However there is a much cooler way to swiftly get to a particular slide while you're presenting. And you don't have to leave Slide Show View. The key is to know thy keyboard shortcuts while presenting. If you have access to a mouse, the easiest thing is to right-click or press Shift+F10 to bring up the shortcut menu. On it, you'll see an entry called Go To Slide. It pops out to show you a list of your slides. Just select the slide title and PowerPoint takes you there. As an aside, creating descriptive titles for your slides makes it easier to identify them in the list.

Alternatively, if you really know your slides, you can actually just type the slide number and press Enter. PowerPoint jumps to that slide. If you have a whole lot of slides, you also can bring up the All Slides dialog box by pressing Ctrl+S. Then you can scroll through your slides by title. The dialog box is easier to work with than the pop-out menu if you have a really big presentation.

Ctrl+T is another handy keyboard shortcut to know if you have to switch to another application. This shortcut brings up the Taskbar. Again, you don't have to leave Slide Show View, so no one has to know how messy your Windows desktop really is.

One last note, if you've completely freaked out and forgotten all of these keyboard shortcuts, press the F1 key for a complete list. And calm down; it's only PowerPoint.

Using Multiple Slide Masters in PowerPoint

PowerPoint uses "masters" to store underlying design elements, such as placeholders, fonts, and background graphics. For example, if you want to put your logo on every slide, you'd put it in the slide master instead of inserting it on each slide individually. You also would make any global font changes in the master, rather than changing each slide. Intelligently using masters can save you a tremendous amount of time.

For years, PowerPoint users whined that you could not have more than one slide master in a presentation. However, in PowerPoint XP and later versions, now you can use multiple masters in one presentation. This enhancement dramatically increases your design flexibility. For example, now you could make different sections of your presentation have different background designs.

In any version of PowerPoint, you access the masters from the View menu. For example, to go to the slide master, you choose View|Master|Slide Master. But now in newer versions, when you are in Master view, you have an extra toolbar and panes. If you want the plain vanilla PowerPoint slide master with the default styles (like the "blank slide" template), click Insert New Slide Master on the Master toolbar. You can then customize this master to your heart's content.

If you want to use a master from a design template instead, again while you are in Slide Master view, click Design on the Formatting toolbar. A pane appears with thumbnails of the various design templates you have available. When you click a thumbnail, you see a small down arrow on the right-hand side. If you click the arrow, you see that one of the options is Add Design, so you can include the design in your presentation.

After you return to Normal view, your masters are available any time you need them. After you add a slide, you can choose to apply a different layout by choosing Format|Slide Design. Once again, the pane appears with your available designs. Click the down arrow and choose Apply to Selected Slide. If you click Apply to All Slides, the new slide master design replaces the old one on all your slides.

Use PowerPoint Notes

Many people like to use PowerPoint's notes feature to create handouts. They are also handy for you as the presenter, since you can put pretty much your whole speech into the Notes if you want. Of course, if you have a lot to say about a particular subject, you may find that some Notes pages end up getting cut off when you print them out.

The problem you run into is that there is only one Note page per slide. You can't just keep typing and typing like you can in Word and hope that PowerPoint will magically flow your text onto more pages. It doesn't work that way.

One way around the problem is to create another slide. If you have a whole lot to say about a topic, that probably means you should break it up into more than one slide anyway. Another way around the problem is to use PowerPoint's AutoFit feature. With AutoFit, PowerPoint reduces the font size to fit the placeholder. Choose Tools|AutoCorrect options and in the AutoFormat As You Type tab, click to add a checkmark next to AutoFit body text to placeholder.

The bad news about this approach is that you can end up with a formatting mess. Mingling a bunch of different font sizes on your Notes pages can make them look ugly and hard to read. For example, one Notes page might use 12-point type and the next uses 9-point type to squash all your verbiage into the box. It's inconsistent at best, and unprofessional-looking at worst.

If you know you will have a lot of notes, a better approach is to modify the underlying Notes page layout. Choose View|Master|Notes Master. You can see that by default, the image of the slide hogs up about half the page. When you click the slide placeholder, handles appear around the edges. Drag a corner handle to make the slide placeholder smaller. You can also increase the size of the text placeholder by clicking and dragging its corner placeholder handles.

If you still can't fit all your Notes, it's probably best to just give up and put them in Word, so you can add pages. Choose File|Send to|Microsoft Word and click the Notes options.

Reducing PowerPoint Bloat

Not too long ago, I had a rather desperate e-mail from a reader who had a strange PowerPoint problem. She had created a basic nine-slide presentation with only a few graphics and a little animation. She couldn't figure out what she did, but the presentation that had been 2 MB, suddenly ballooned up to 59MB. As any veteran PowerPoint user can tell you, the larger a presentation gets, the less stable it becomes. Her presentation had started behaving badly and things weren't looking good.

A few days before, I had a similar problem with a 200K three-slide presentation that inexplicably expanded to 5MB. I was using PowerPoint 2003, which I haven't spent much time with. In my case, I saved my presentation back to an earlier version by choosing File|Save As and selecting a different version from the drop-down. PowerPoint gives you a warning message that if you've done anything that's specific to a newer version it will be lost. I hadn't and I didn't care. I don't remember how many versions I went back, but it was several.

I found out later, my solution may have been overkill. Apparently the Fast Saves option, which has annoyed Word users for years also causes bloat problems in PowerPoint. If you have presentation weirdness, you should choose

Tool|Options|Save and remove the checkmark next to Fast Saves if it's there. Then save the presentation with a new name.

As it turned out, the reader had imported a large image into her presentation, so it wasn't really PowerPoint's fault that it bloated up. When you work with PowerPoint, you need to think about the images you insert. If the presentation is going to be viewed on screen, no image ever needs to be more than 72 or 96 dpi. You also generally would never have an image with dimensions larger than 1024 x 768, which is the resolution most laptops run at these days.

Those people who just randomly import 5 megapixel digital camera photos without modifying them first are in for a big PowerPoint surprise. You can scale an image in PowerPoint, so it looks small. But if you bring a 40MB image into PowerPoint, it will increase your presentation by at least 40MB no matter how small it looks on the slide. The answer is to use your image editing program to size your images appropriately before adding them into your presentation.

In newer versions of PowerPoint, you also can use PowerPoint's built-in compression feature to help shrink images (and your presentation size). Just right-click the image and choose Format Picture and press the Compress button. Now change the resolution to Web/Screen and click OK. A message appears asking if you really want to compress your pictures. Click Apply then OK. Now resave the presentation and you will find it's a lot smaller.

Packing Up PowerPoint

When you give a presentation, you want your audience thinking about what you are saying, not what program you used to create your slides. After your presentation is finalized, you can save it as a show that runs without the need for you to go into PowerPoint. This way, you don't have to open PowerPoint and choose View| Slide Show to run your presentation. Instead, the show runs automatically when you open the file. Slide show files are saved with a different file extension (.PPS) than regular PowerPoint files (.PPT).

1. Choose File|Open and click the Look in drop down box to find the folder your presentation is located in. Double-click the filename to open the presentation.

2. Choose File|Save As.

3. Change the Save as Type drop-down box to PowerPoint show. You can either leave the default file name (which is your presentation filename with a .PPS extension) or type a new one.

4. Click Save. The file is saved to your hard disk with the filename you specified. If you look at the file in Windows Explorer, you see that it has a "show" icon, instead of the regular PowerPoint file icon.

If you want to run your show from your desktop, open Windows Explorer. Find your new PowerPoint show on your hard disk. Right-click and choose Send To Desktop (create shortcut). Right-click your new shortcut and choose Rename to give the shortcut a more user-friendly name. Double-click the icon to run the show.

Note that if you decide to change your presentation later, you need to save it as a slide show again in order to run it from the slide show file. Follow steps 1 and 2 and in step 3 be sure to save the new .PPS file with the same name as the old one. When PowerPoint asks if you want to replace the existing file, click Yes.

Not everyone owns PowerPoint, so if you want to package your slide show up and take it somewhere, you can use PowerPoint's Pack and Go feature. In PowerPoint 2003, this feature is called Package for CD. Either way, the tool gathers all the files you need together along with the PowerPoint Presentation Viewer. With the Viewer, even people without PowerPoint can run your show.

Choose File|Pack and Go (or File|Package for CD in 2003). Go through the wizard and be sure to tell it you want to include the Viewer.

Export PowerPoint Graphics

Not all of us are blessed with an unlimited array of software. Some folks have to make do with what they can afford or what the boss will agree to purchase for them. So I've met a number of people who basically use PowerPoint as their sole drawing program. It's really not as bad as it sounds, since PowerPoint does have a number of drawing tools that are quite sophisticated once you learn how they work.

However, sometimes you want to move your pictures out of PowerPoint. So how do you get them off the slide? Your first option is to see if you can copy the graphic. First click to select the graphic and choose Draw|Ungroup. Then choose Draw|Regroup. This process converts the graphic to a PowerPoint object, if it isn't already. In fact, sometimes you'll see a dialog box asking whether you want to convert the graphic. (Say "yes" if it asks.)

Now open the program where you want to copy the graphic. Switch to PowerPoint, select the graphic, and click Edit|Copy. Now switch back to your other program and choose Edit|Paste or ideally Edit|Paste Special (if the option exists). If you can use Paste Special, choose Windows Metafile, Metafile, or Enhanced Metafile if you have an option as to the type of picture you want to paste. Your PowerPoint image should appear in the other program.

Alternatively, you can export the entire slide. In PowerPoint, choose File|Save As. In the Save As Type drop-down box, choose the graphic format type you want to save in (WMF, BMP, JPG, PNG, GIF, or TIF), give the file a name, and click OK. PowerPoint asks whether you want to export just the current slide or your entire presentation. Answer No to export just the current slide.

The exported slide file can then be imported into another program just like any other graphic file. In fact, this technique is often used to import a specialized slide back into PowerPoint at times when you want just one or a few slides that don't look anything like the currently selected template. It's basically a sneaky way around PowerPoint's one-template per presentation limitation.

Make Your Presentations Look Good

A good presentation design reflects well on the presenter, but, unfortunately, the converse is also true. If your design is amateurish or garish, your audience won't think much of the presentation as a whole. Good design should enhance rather than detract from your message. In fact, the best designs are the ones you don't really notice. Too much visual clutter tends to confuse and annoy an audience, so keep your designs simple. Make sure every design element you add has a logical reason for being on the slide. For example, you may want to use graphics to support a point or to visually convey conceptual relationships. Adding random graphics just because you can often doesn't work out well.

1. Use White Space Effectively

In design, what you don't add to a space is as important as what you do add. In graphic design parlance, empty space is called "white space" and it's an important part of your layout. Leave enough white space around slide objects to keep the slide from getting too cluttered and difficult to read.

2. Be Consistent

Colors, graphics, backgrounds and other slide elements should be used consistently. PowerPoint makes this easy to do using the its Masters (see Chapter 6). Every title should look like every other title and slide background should be the same throughout, except when you have a reason to change it, such as for a title slide or to indicate an introduction of a new topic.

3. Exercise Restraint

PowerPoint has so many tools, it's easy to go a little crazy with fonts, graphics, animations, transitions, and sound. Resist the urge to throw in every possible effect or color in the PowerPoint palette. Add these items only when they add to the message you are trying to convey.

4. Choose Appropriate Graphics

The world is full of cheesy graphics. Think before you throw in that "kinda cool" free graphic you found on the Internet. You want to appear professional and if the graphic doesn't strengthen your presentation, don't use it. Remember that the purpose of your presentation is to convey information, not to show off snazzy graphics.

5. Choose Color Wisely

Color has an emotional impact, so be careful how you use it. For example, the color red is often used to convey danger (think Stop signs, for example), so exercise caution when you use it. In addition certain colors, such as red and green are difficult for color-blind people to distinguish, so be careful in using these colors.

6. Choose Appropriate Typefaces

There are two main types of fonts: serif and sans-serif. Serif fonts are typestyles such as Times New Roman that have little "tails." Sans-serif literally means without serif, and include fonts such as Arial, which have no "tails." In printed documents, serif fonts are generally easier to read, but in a presentation the cleaner lines of sans serif fonts are often easier to see, especially in a large room. If you are in doubt, create a quickie slide that uses the fonts you are considering and project it on a wall. Stand in the back of the room and see how well you can read it. Another thing to keep in mind: when you select typefaces, don't use more than two on a slide. If it's a formal presentation, also avoid flowery decorative typefaces. Try to stick with fonts that go well with your overall company image.

About the Author
Susan C. Daffron

Susan Daffron is the president of Logical Expressions, Inc. a book and software publishing company in Sandpoint, Idaho.

In addition to the Logical Tips books, she is the author of:

- *Vegan Success: Scrumptious, Healthy Vegan Recipes for Busy People,*

- *Web Business Success: The Entrepreneur's Guide to Web Sites That Work,*

- *Happy Hound: Develop a Great Relationship with Your Adopted Dog or Puppy,* and

- *Happy Tabby: Develop a Great Relationship with Your Adopted Cat or Kitten.*

A recognized expert on Web, editorial, design, and publishing topics, in addition to her books Susan has written more than 70 articles that have appeared in national magazines, more than 200 print newspaper articles, an online software training course, a mainstream software book, book chapters, and countless online articles. She also is the co-creator of a writing and creativity software program called IdeaWeaver.

Along with her writing, Susan has been doing design and editorial work since 1989. She has created magazines, newsletters, books and other book-length documents such as users guides and manuals. She was awarded the Most Valuable Professional designation from Microsoft in 1996 for her expertise in working with long documents in Microsoft Word..

Share Tips with Friends

If you like this book, share the Logical Tips books with your friends!

Order Form

Qty	Title	Price	Total
	Logical Tips for Mastering Your Computer	$14.95	
	Logical Tips for Mastering the Internet	$14.95	
	Logical Tips for Mastering Microsoft Office	$14.95	
	Logical Tips for Mastering Microsoft Windows	$14.95	
	Shipping & Handling - $4.60 for first book, $1.00 for each additional book for US Priority Mail within the U.S.*		

____ Check enclosed with order

____ Please charge my credit card [ ] Visa   [ ] Master Card

Number: _____

Name on Card: _____ Exp. Date: _____

Buyer's Name:_____

Buyer's Address: _____

Shipping Address (if different):_____

_____

Please fax to 208-265-0956 or mail with your payment to:

Logical Expressions, Inc.

311 Fox Glen Road, Sandpoint, ID 83864

* *Please contact us for more information on orders mailed outside of the U.S. (Our number is 208-265-6147)*

Breinigsville, PA USA
18 August 2009

222539BV00002B/223/A